GEORGE JONAS

THE JONAS VARIATIONS

A Literary Seance

Canada Council
for the Arts

Conseil des Arts
du Canada

ONTARIO ARTS COUNCIL
CONSEIL DES ARTS DE L'ONTARIO

Canadian
Heritage

Patrimoine
canadien

Canadä

The publisher gratefully acknowledges the support of the Canada Council for the
Arts and the Ontario Arts Council for its publishing program. We acknowledge the
financial support of the Government of Canada through the Canada Book Fund
(CBF) for our publishing activities, and the Government of Ontario through the
Ontario Media Development Corporation, an agency of the Ontario Ministry of
Culture, and the Ontario Book Publishing Tax Credit Program.

Reasonable efforts have been made to locate copyright holders for materials
contained herein. Parties wishing to identify copyright holders for works
in this volume should contact the publisher.

LIBRARY AND ARCHIVES CANADA CATALOGUING IN PUBLICATION

Jonas, George, 1935–
The Jonas variations : a literary seance / George Jonas.

Poems.
ISBN 978-1-77086-056-8

I. Title.

PS8519.O5J66 2011   C811′.54   C2011-904037-9

Cover design: Angel Guerra/Archetype
Interior text design: Tannice Goddard, Soul Oasis Networking
Printer: Sunville Printco Inc.

Printed and bound in Canada.

MIX
Paper from
responsible sources
FSC® C014078

CORMORANT BOOKS INC.
215 SPADINA AVENUE, STUDIO 230, TORONTO, ONTARIO, CANADA M5T 2C7
www.cormorantbooks.com

CONTENTS

USER'S GUIDE

～

THIS IS A BOOK of lives and poems remembered. I had to write my other books before I could read them, but this one I had to read before I could write it. And so I did, over the years, starting as a teenager. My interest was not always literary.

"Dad, any chance for a few coins this weekend? I've a heavy date."

My father was sympathetic but insolvent. We were in postwar Budapest in the early 1950s, behind what Sir Winston had dubbed the Iron Curtain. Stalin was still alive.

"With your Bolshevik friends in charge, I'm afraid you'll have to subsidize your own sex life." My father sounded grumpy because he was. The Communist takeover had him ruined, but my friends and I had fashionably joined the Young Communist League.

"Dad, er ... see that pristine copy of *Kabala und Liebe*? What if I took it to the antiquarian? It should fetch me a night out, and you never read Schiller anyway."

"Do you?"

"Well, not *Kabala und Liebe*."

"You should," my father said. "It's one of Schiller's best plays, better than *Wilhelm Tell*. Verdi based the libretto of *Luisa Miller* on it — at least Salvatore Cammarano did." A former baritone of the *Wiener Staatsoper*, the Viennese Opera, Father could pull librettists' names out of a hat. "Tell you what. Read it first, then you can sell it."

I did and I did. Schiller's play and my date both turned out to be memorable — my date more so at the time, the play in retrospect. As a bourgeois bohemian, Father believed young people should satisfy their bodies simultaneously with their souls.

A child's entry to the world of letters is mediated through the minds of adults. In my case, the adults were the inhabitants of my parents' bookcases. Some spirits displayed themselves in wood-and-glass cabinets inside pristine first editions, but most reposed between smudged, frayed, uncut, even dog-eared covers. A few now inhabit this book — not as translations, scholarly or otherwise, but as spectres in a kind of literary seance. Think of me as a medium conjuring up spirits in a series of inspirations, imitations, salutations, reverberations and sometimes refutations.

The Jonas Variations is my tribute to fifty poets who wrote in languages other than English, complete with irreverent — but I hope not inaccurate — thumbnail sketches of their public and private lives. Literary history acknowledges some as major poets and takes a lesser view of others; I selected them not because of their standing but because they stayed with me. English-speaking readers glancing at the table of contents will recognize the names of about half, and not even their compatriots will recognize all.

Reading a poem in a language other than English does not make me want to translate it, but it may awaken an urge in me to put English words in the poet's mouth. Not necessarily the

English equivalents of the words the poet used, but whatever English words the poem inspired in me, if "inspire" is the word. As urges go, mine is pretty minor; but even though it falls well short of an obsession, over the years I have made no effort to resist it. What you see in these pages is the result.

Some may consider *The Jonas Variations* an anthology of translations. I do not and here is why. Once I watched a commercial director set up a fashion shoot at St. Mark's Square in Venice. "Look at those pigeons," he said to his assistant. "I love them, but do me a favour. Get rid of the grey ones."

Unless you feel equal to the task of separating grey pigeons from their multi-coloured flocks, you are not ready to separate poems from their languages. A translation means retaining everything, except the original words. They are the grey pigeons. The medal goes to the translator who can chase off the grey pigeons, while making sure the white, red, and blue-bar ones stay put in the square. They are poetry.

The trouble is, they rarely stay put. They fly away with the grey pigeons. No wonder poetry is traditionally defined as whatever is lost in translation.

Sometimes, amazingly, poetry remains. The grey pigeons fly off and the white ones stay in the square. No one can explain it. It is a miracle: St. Mark's covered in snow. I have never felt daring enough to count on it.

So what, then, do you do with a poem in a foreign language? Well, you can read it, enjoy it, and get on with your life. But if you feel you must do something, as I did, try a free translation. A free translation has a better chance of becoming a poem, but less of remaining a translation. If it is free enough, it may liberate itself altogether from being a translation, and simply turn into a poem in one language inspired by a poem in another. In this collection there are several.

An adaptation is different. I define it as a literary work that treats another as raw material, a departure point, something to acknowledge and build on, the way one builds on any life experience. To adapt a poem, it is unnecessary for it to have been written in a foreign language. You can adapt a Shakespeare sonnet, using it as raw material for your own, if you have the nerve. Don't try it at home.

A variation — again, in my definition — is conjuring up another poet's theme and developing it in your own manner. A reader familiar with the original may or may not recognize it. Unlike adaptations, variations rarely borrow whole narratives, but they are often your fancy of what the original poet would have written if s/he had been writing in English. This makes variations a closer kin to divinations than to translations.

The opposite of variation is imitation. It is something a poet writes in the manner of another. Imitation has often been called the sincerest form of flattery. In poems written in imitation, the theme may be different, but the voice is unmistakably the poet's who is being flattered. A poet may not recognize being skillfully adapted or varied, but should recognize being imitated.

A reverberation is an echo of a poem, usually faint and distant, often highly evocative. A refutation, as the name implies, is a poetic dispute. Whether tribute, translation, adaptation, imitation or variation, turning to one poem to inform another is usually an expression of homage. They all are, in this collection.

The only claim I make for the original poems that sparked the poems in this book is that I like them. I do not suggest that they are necessarily the most beautiful or most influential poems in their own language. Many have no "originals," strictly speaking; they are my homage to a poet's spirit written in his manner, or a variation on his theme. What I claim is that these spirits and their words have seduced me over the years. Having impregnated my mind, as it were, they demanded birth, or rather re-birth, in English. To have come to my attention, each had to have been written in a language I could either read or at least decipher. No doubt, magnificent poems have been written in Cree, Gujarati, Mandarin and Malay — poems that would have dazzled and influenced me had I been able to read them, but I could not. This collection demarcates my linguistic boundaries. German came to me in the nursery; Hungarian in the schoolyard; Russian and Latin in the classroom; French and Italian in hotel lobbies and restaurants; and finally English, which did not come to me at all until I went to it.

To repeat, I do not offer *The Jonas Variations* as a book of translations, because that word implies a higher degree of fidelity to both form and content than I feel justified in claiming for any poem in this book. What I am submitting to the reader is some poems in English, echoing poems in other languages. Such adaptations or reverberations can be enjoyed without knowing how much, or how little, they resemble their sources; but if I picked up a book of this kind I would like to have the information available. Translations often miss the poetry, but it is possible for poetry to miss the translation. In scholarly works the non-bilingual reader has to take it on faith that the prosaic and awkward Omar Khayyám-text he is reading in English (sample line: *with futility we try, exert, weep, or keen*) is really a poem in Farsi, while in free adaptations like Edward Fitzgerald's *Rubaiyat*, the reader may wonder if the delightful English poem he is reading (same line: "Nor all your Tears wash out a Word of it") has anything to do with Omar Khayyám. Some readers may be interested in this to the exclusion of everything else and some may not care about it at all; my aim was to offer a glimpse to curious readers by illustrating the process with selected originals in German, French, Italian, Hungarian and Latin, without overwhelming those who were not interested.

Sometimes people want to know what the fuss is all about. We keep saying "poets" — well, who and what are they? Opinions are divided. The American poet Joyce Kilmer (1886–1918) believed that poets are fools who create second-best things like poems because they cannot create really lovely things like trees. "I think that I shall never see/ A poem lovely as a tree" Kilmer began his most-anthologized poem shortly after the turn of the century — not this century, but the one before — ending it with: "*Poems are made by fools like me/ but only God can make a tree.*"

I remember wondering when I read this: are poem-makers fools like Kilmer? The likely answer is: fools, maybe, but fools like Kilmer, probably not. Judging by their life stories, they are fools like themselves. They can be passionate fools, patriotic fools, sensual fools and arid fools; they can be fools of conviction or fools of confusion. They can be handsome, romantic fools who resemble Lord Byron and nerdy, hirsute, bespectacled fools who do not. They can be, in the words of the tenth century Arab poet Abu Ala'a al-Maari, "believing and unbelieving fools."

To be a fool, though, is not enough. As Alexander Pope pointed out almost three centuries ago:

> Sir, I admit your general rule,
> That every poet is a fool,
> But you yourself may serve to show it,
> That every fool is not a poet.

What do these weird wordsmiths who look at us solemnly from paintings or daguerreotypes have in common? Instead of offering my own answer, here is Rainer Maria Rilke's:

> O sage, Dichter, was du tust? — Ich rühme.
> Aber das Tödliche und Ungetüme,
> wie haltst du's aus, wie nimmst du's hin? — Ich rühme.
> Aber das Namenlose, Anonyme,
> wie rufst du's, Dichter, dennoch an? — Ich rühme.
> Woher dein Recht, in jeglichem Kostüme,
> in jeder Maske wahr zu sein? — Ich rühme.
> Und dass das Stille und das Ungestüme
> wie Stern und Sturm dich kennen?: — Weil ich rühme

In English I hear it as:

> Tell us, poet, what do you do? — I praise.
> And if you were to meet a hateful gaze,
> a monstrous face. a deadly touch? — I praise.
> Assume you're lost. Entangled in a maze.
> See only sameness, emptiness. — I praise.
> But what gives you the right? Can you erase
> the truth? Or mask, or dress it up? — I praise.
> Have stars and storms their own peculiar ways
> of recognizing you? — They hear me praise.

The reader will note that most poems in *The Jonas Variations* are rhymed and metred, despite a tendency in modern English poetry to write "free verse" — that is, a preference for poetic devices other than rhymes and accentual rhythms. There are two reasons for my resistance to "freedom" in this book. Most of the original poems that inspired me are rhymed and metred. And I like rhymes and metres. I think they work in English as well as in any other language. Rhymes, far from being bells on a clown's costume — as T. S. Eliot, no mean rhymester himself, dismissed them — are more like wheels on a cart. It is possible to pull a cart without wheels, but you had better quadruple the donkeys. It is perfectly feasible to write poetry without metre or rhyme, but "free" verse, far from being free, requires many times the effort and ingenuity to come close to casting the same spell and being as evocative, memorable, inevitable, and harmonious as metred, rhyming verse can be simply by virtue of using those devices.

When asked the purpose of poetry, Confucius replied that it helped people to learn the names of plants and such, and to remember them. I would have said that poetry helps what you want to say to have the ring of truth. Before something rings true, however, it is useful for it to ring. This, in brief, is my case for rhymes and metres.

Last but not least, I would like to underline that I am not on a cultural mission to introduce Latin or Italian or German or Hungarian or Russian or French poetry to English-speaking readers, nor am I on an aesthetic mission to promote "traditional" poetry that rhymes, scans, or tinkles. I am not on a mission of any kind. I simply enjoy reading poetry in other languages, and over the years some poems I read inspired me to write what I hope are a few enjoyable poems in English.

George Jonas
Toronto, the summer of 2011

POETS, IN ORDER OF APPEARANCE

THE SEANCE

Apollinaire

WITH A NOD TO the alphabet, let us conjure up Guillame Apollinaire first, an Italian-born Pole who became a major French poet. People who are surprised by this should remember that to be a French poet the important thing is not to be born French (though it helps) but to be born a poet. Born poets have far more leeway to decide whether they would be French than born Frenchmen have to decide whether they would be poets.

Wilhelm Albert Vladimir Apollinaris Kostrowicki, born into a cosmopolitan-aristocratic-bohemian family residing in Rome in 1880, decided to be French twenty years later when he settled in Paris and assumed the name of Apollinaire. In the vanguard of many modern movements from Cubism to Surrealism — a word he coined — and close friend to such icons of modernity as Jean Cocteau, Pablo Picasso, and Marc Chagall, Apollinaire survived a serious shrapnel wound while serving with the French army in World War I. This enabled him to succumb to the Spanish flu at the age of thirty-eight on November 9, 1918.

"Autumn crocuses" is based on Apollinaire's much-anthologized poem, "*Les Colchiques.*" I wrote the English version years ago at

17

the request of my friend Stephen Vizinczey, author of *In Praise of Older Women*, who wanted to use the first three lines of the poem as an epigraph for his novel *An Innocent Millionaire* but could find no English translation to suit him. After rendering

Le pré est vénéneux mais joli en automne
Les vaches y paissant
Lentement s'empoisonnent

as

Cobalt meadows sprout poisoned flowers
envenoming wet cows that graze
late into false fall's frosty showers

for Vizinczey, I thought I might as well continue and pretzel into English the whole poem. It's a celebration rather than a translation of the original, but readers who can decipher French may decide that I took too many liberties even for a celebration, and cancel my poetic licence.

AUTUMN CROCUSES

Cobalt meadows sprout poisoned flowers
envenoming wet cows that graze
late into false fall's frosty showers.
Autumn crocuses bloom in blue,
like your violet, dream-soaked gaze,
soft petals of a baneful hue,
eyes slowly poisoning my days.

Accordion cue. Capes. A swarm
of schoolboys plucks and demolishes
crocus daughters (who are their own mother crocuses)
as blue as your eyes that flutter in alarm
the way windblown wild flowers quiver.

The herdsman's chant is next, as he begins to wind
his way, with lowing cows steaming behind,
leaving the great moribund field forever.

LES COLCHIQUES

Le pré est vénéneux mais joli en automne
Les vaches y paissant
Lentement s'empoisonnent
Le colchique couleur de cerne et de lilas
Y fleurit tes yeux sont comme cette fleur-la
Violatres comme leur cerne et comme cet automne
Et ma vie pour tes yeux lentement s'empoisonne

Les enfants de l'école viennent avec fracas
Vêtus de hoquetons et jouant de l'harmonica
Ils cueillent les colchiques qui sont comme des mères
Filles de leurs filles et sont couleur de tes paupières
Qui battent comme les fleurs battent au vent dément

Le gardien du troupeau chante tout doucement
Tandis que lentes et meuglant les vaches abandonnent
Pour toujours ce grand pré mal fleuri par l'automne

Verlaine

DASHING TO THE OTHER end of the alphabet takes us to the next
virtuoso, Paul Verlaine. This one, elected France's "Prince of Poets"
in 1894 by his admiring peers, was fortunate to have lived in a period
when bohemians were worshipped for their liabilities as much
as for their assets, their vices as much as for their virtues. Verlaine
was awash with both, his magnificent spirit of a poet having been
encased in the body and central nervous system of a disease-
ridden dysfunctional alcoholic bisexual lecher. During his eventful
life he spent some time in jail for shooting and injuring the
boy with whom he had a passionate affair, and who is remembered
as a great French poet in his own right, Arthur Rimbaud. Need-
less to say, Verlaine is equally noted for the power and beauty
of his work, including the poems he wrote for people he later
abandoned or tried to kill (e.g. "*La bonne chanson*," written to the
wife he deserted, Mathilde Mauté de Fleurville). Born in 1844, the
absinthe-guzzling genius died at fifty-two, in 1896.

Here is "Moonlight," a fairly straightforward (albeit free) trans-
lation of Verlaine's well-known "*Clair de lune*":

MOONLIGHT

A strange landscape, your soul.
Revelers wearing masks,
one strums a high-strung lute:
merry beat, mournful tune.

Lovers and bon vivants.
They sing in minor keys
moonlight's calm melodies.
Listen, but don't be fooled.

As midnight comes sinister,
your soulscape, turning dark,
bursts into tears, like her sister
fountains, slim, in the park.

The poem I call "Innocent Boys" uses Verlaine's "*Les Ingénus*" merely as a platform from which to launch my own flight of fancy — a variation on Verlaine's theme, if you will. The original, which I reproduce below, has worthy English translations and interested readers may wish to look them up. (Personally, I like Louis Simpson's. It is a genuine translation as well as a poem in English. He renders the title as "The Young Fools.")

LES INGÉNUS

Les hauts talons luttaient avec les longues jupes,
En sorte que, selon le terrain et le vent,
Parfois luisaient des bas de jambes, trop souvent
Interceptés—et nous aimions ce jeu de dupes.

INNOCENT BOYS

Epic clashes of skirt and shoe remain
unresolved as the odd ankle emerges,
if only here or there, before it merges
with boring hemline's undulating plain.

Parfois aussi le dard d'un insecte jaloux
Inquiétait le col des belles sous les branches,
Et c'était des éclairs soudains de nuques blanches,
Et ce régal comblait nos jeunes yeux de fous.

Our childish hearts rejoice as sunset smoulders
and red mosquitoes dive in bold advances
on white necks from green twilights: tiny lances.
Alarmed beauties flash blinding shoulders.

Le soir tombait, un soir équivoque d'automne:
Les belles, se pendant rêveuses à nos bras,
Dirent alors des mots si spécieux, tout bas,
Que notre âme depuis ce temps tremble et s'étonne.

Shadows grow, autumns come. We tremble.
The beauties take our arms, we walk for hours,
speak in riddles, sense enigmatic powers.
Our souls shiver in splendour still. Remember?

Dante

LET'S START WITH THE poem. The speaker is Gianciotto Malatesta, addressing us from his permanent residence in Inferno.

SNAKE IN BRONZE

When I was young and none too smart
I made the odd mistake.
One I recall was putting
On a pedestal a snake.
A naturally pretty snake
Born near a cottage, by a lake.

Doing what snakes do well, she shed
Her lovers, as she shed her skin,
I'd find gruesome bits now and then
And throw them in a garbage bin.

She lived in a magic carpet that I
Had bought for her and wrapped her in.
Can't answer if you ask me why.

Well-versed in snakedom's gentle art
She sneaked in and out of my heart
Slithered in and out of my carpet:
Anything straight, she'd bend or warp it.

We lived together and apart.

Last night I saw her back in town
Looking demure in her evening gown
Having advanced from a pretty snake
Born near a cottage, by a lake
To nothing less than a baroness,
With a crest, a keep, and an address.

When I was young and none too smart
I made the odd mistake.
One was thinking a second bite
Cures the first bite of a snake.
But if the first fang is a curse
The second's venom is much worse.

Remind me, if you are a friend,
Of snakebite's progeny and pain

Lest I relapse and clasp an asp
To my bosom again.

"Snake in Bronze" is my variation on a theme by Dante Alighieri (*1265–1321*). My "snake" is Dante's memorable Francesca da Rimini, but not as the author of *The Divine Comedy* represents her in "Inferno": mesmerizing, uplifting, extolling the power of love. In my version she is portrayed as she may have appeared to her husband, the crippled Gianciotto Malatesta, residing in another circle of hell. Gianciotto ended up in the nether region not so much for killing Francesca, since killing an adulterous wife was not necessarily a burning offence, but for killing her lover, the handsome Paolo Malatesta, Gianciotto's own brother. Slaying a rival sibling in Dante's time, though much indulged in, did make you risk becoming an infernal roommate of Cain.

Giving a forum to another voice from hell seems fair to me. As a contemporary, Dante may have been biased: Italy's greatest poet was closer to the ruling family of Ravenna, the Polentas, whose daughter was Francesca, than to the ruling family of Rimini, the Malatestas, one of whose sons killed her. Dante actually spent his last years in the Ravenna home of Francesca's nephew, Guido Novello da Polenta — and may himself have met Paolo Malatesta, the other victim, in Florence some years earlier. This may have influenced him to view the beautiful lovers in a more sympathetic light than the possessive cripple who slaughtered them. Dante does not appear to take Francesca's offence seriously, though he is still prudent enough to put her in the second circle of hell. After all, she did commit adultery, a misdeed it would not have been politically correct to make light of in the fourteenth century (c. 1310–14) when the poet composed *La Divina Commedia*. Back then people still took the idea of marriage and their vows seriously.

My variation on the theme is the fratricidal Gianciotto's version of Francesca. Self-serving as it may be, it seems no more far-fetched than the exculpatory legends that grew up around the Polenta family's libidinous daughter. The latter include a tale by none other than Giovanni Boccaccio (1313–1375). In Boccaccio's fable, offered after Dante' death, Francesca innocently marries hideous Gianciotto under false pretenses, having been tricked into believing that she would be marrying Paolo the Fair.

Not so, say others. Gianciotto, especially, denounces Boccaccio's story as a rumour spread by his enemies. "Arrant nonsense," he told me when I interviewed him in fiery *Caina*, his circle of hell.

I can't offer an Italian version of this interview for obvious reasons, so I'll offer Dante's inscription on the archway to Inferno instead, coupled with the way it sounds to me in English:

"Per me si va ne la città dolente,
Per me si va ne l'etterno dolore
Per me si va tra la perduta gente.

"My portals lead to the city of anguish
where undying the damned, lackluster, lustrous,
in doleful circles of perdition languish.

Giustizia mosse il mio alto fattore;
Fecemi la divina podestate,
La somma sapienza e 'l primo amore

 The divine quest for redress and justice
 extends to all, without mercy's veneer,
 wisdom and primal love, for which God's lust is

Dinanzi a me non fuor cose create
Se non etterne, e io etterno duro.
Lasciate ogne speranza, voi ch'intrate."

 unquenchable. In my eternal sphere
 what has been is and will forever be.
 Leave all hope at the gate who enter here."

My personal memory of the *Inferno* dates back to the winter of 1944–45. Budapest was under siege. Adults with functioning limbs were foraging for food. The old lady sharing our air raid shelter — at least she seemed very old to me at the time — was once married to the fine Hungarian novelist, Gyula Krúdy. She wanted to know what I was reading whenever she saw me, which was all too often, and was never satisfied with my answer. My reading habits seemed hopelessly lowbrow to her.

One day I happened to be reading an adventure story by Karl May when she accosted me. The German Zane Grey, May had spent much of his life in jail where he wrote immensely popular western-style juvenilia, tailor-made for nine-year-olds like me.

"Isn't that interesting." Mrs. Krúdy raised her lorgnette to inspect me as she might an alien life form. "Karl May, did you say? My late husband was reading Dante at nine."

She sailed on, as much as one can sail in an air raid shelter. When my father returned from foraging I asked him if we had any books by someone named Dante. He wanted to know why. While I was telling him, the Russian artillery pounded our besieged city. The walls of the underground shelter shook. We noticed white mist seeping underneath the steel door from a phosphorous bomb that landed in the street outside. Miraculously, it did not ignite.

"Don't worry, son," my father said when I finished. "When Mrs. Krúdy's husband was nine, he had to go to Dante to read about the *Inferno*. For you, hell is making a housecall."

Goethe, von

THERE ARE THOSE WHO view Johann Wolfgang von Goethe (1749–1832) as the greatest German poet who ever lived, one of the immortals of world literature; then there are those who consider him a self-centred, pompous windbag. The two positions are so firmly held as almost to amount to schools of thought. They always puzzled me, because I never saw much dichotomy between them. I could see no reason for the greatest German poet, an immortal of world literature, not to be a self-centred pompous windbag at the same time. In fact, I could view being a pompous windbag, if not a requirement for the job of a great poet, at least an occupational hazard.

Since I am unlikely to resolve the dispute in these notes, I will say no more about it. Goethe was born in the eighteenth century and died in the nineteenth. He is the progenitor of the romantic movement known as *Sturm und Drang*; he accomplished this by publishing a novel in 1774, *The Sorrows of Young Werther*, which may be described as the first runaway bestseller in Western literature. (Or perhaps the second, after Cervantes' *Don Quixote*.) This could open a fascinating discussion about popular literary characters of past ages that survive, like Don Quixote, the knight of the mournful countenance, and ones that do not, like young Werther and his bloody sorrows. But such a discussion would take us too far afield. In any event, the protagonist of Goethe's magnum opus, *Faust*, survived as well as any character in history.

Here I'm representing the author of *Faust* by four light stanzas. "*Nähe des Geliebten*" sounds more like lyrics for a popular song than a poem by a giant of world literature, and indeed it has been set to music by more nineteenth century composers than you could shake a stick at, including my father (Georg M. Hübsch, 1883–1972). I could not get Father's melody out of my mind, so I translated the text. The English words resemble the German words, in a ballpark sort of way, and they fit my father's tune just as well. German-speaking readers might enjoy looking at the original.

NEAR THE BELOVED

I think of you,
   when sunset paints the seashore
a crimson hue,
and when the moon
   spreads salve on the abrasion,
I think of you.

It's you I see,
   when clouds of dust are whirling
high on a ridge,
or when I look
   at rippling waves returning
beneath a bridge.

I hear your voice
   in the rumble of thunder:
a voice I will
listen to as
   the summer nights meander
and all is still.

I'm at your side.
   No matter what the distance,

you're always near;
as stars replace
    the sun without resistance,
would you were here.

NÄHE DES GELIEBTEN

Ich denke dein,
  Wenn mir der Sonne schimmer
Vom Meere strahlt;
Ich denke dein,
  Wenn sich des Mondes Flimmer
In Quellen malt.

Ich sehe dich,
  Wenn auf dem fernen Wege
Der Staub sich hebt,
In tiefer Nacht,
  Wenn auf dem schmalen Stege
Der Wandrer bebt.

Ich höre dich,
  Wenn dort mit dumpfem Rauschen
Die Welle steigt.
Im stillen Haine
  geh' ich oft zu lauschen,
Wenn alles schweigt.

Ich bin bei dir,
  Du seist auch noch so ferne,

Du bist mir nah!
Die Sonne sinkt,
    bald leuchten mir die Sterne.
O wärst du da!

Goethe's night songs of wayfarers — *Wandrer's Nachtlieder* — of which he wrote several, are often classified as nature poems (*Naturgedichte*) but they are really romantic conceits, musing about the earthly journey of mortals. In the fall of 1780, in a Thuringian hunting shack, Goethe pencilled into a notebook the most famous of them, ending with the lines "*Warte nur, balde/ Ruhest du auch*" ("Just wait, soon/ You too will rest") quoted more than any other line of German poetry throughout the nineteenth century. I chose to enlarge on his eight-line miniature because I just couldn't stop and because I knew there was not a damn thing Goethe could do about it.

SIMILAR

Over the peaks
The sun descends
In slow degrees.
The evening comes.
The summer ends.
A feeble breeze
Carries away
A bird's last song.

Soft shadows play
Among the trees.
Sparse woods decay,
Thick peats decline
In mottled brown.
The wind dies down.
The world's at peace.

The layered skies
Far in the west
Crimson and rust.
A glowing disc
With clouds still white

Reigns sovereign
Then slowly sinks.
Everything fits
The master plan.
Nothing is wrong.
The day is dead,
Long live the night.

In fading light
Walk on and trust
A stubborn, strong
Quixotic quest,
Your wanderlust.
Pilgrims arrive
Where they belong.
You, too, will rest.
It won't be long.

Heredia

JOSÉ MARÍA DE HEREDIA Y Giraud (1842–1905) had one ambition in life: to write the perfect sonnet. Anyone whose aim is perfection is doomed to failure, but in "The Flight of the Centaurs" Heredia came close. The sonnet may not be perfect — an ideal that cannot be achieved, by definition — but I have never seen anything as near to perfection as those fourteen lines. Whenever I read them, I feel shivers down my spine.

The spine is a divining rod for poetry. It is more reliable than academic analysis. It is tingling sensations, not learned discourse, that reveal the presence of greatness beneath the verbiage. Heredia concealed much greatness under very little verbiage — his 1893 book *Les Trophées* is his only volume — but as a charter member of the *Parnassiens*, the school of French formalists, he was keen on academic theory. Luckily, it did not stifle his formidable natural gifts.

Formalist poets of Heredia's persuasion (Paul Verlaine, Leconte de Lisle, and Sully-Prudhomme were among the other stellar names) tried to feel little, write little, publish little, but ponder and tinker a lot. This somewhat monkish attitude did not hurt the genuinely talented among them, and served a useful social function by keeping the less talented under a lid. It wasn't until the let-it-all-hang-out 1960s, with its dreadful junk inundating the bookstores, that one gained real appreciation for the cloistered habits of the Parnassists. In their sparse, hierarchical, anti-spontaneous, and highly structured space they approached the creative process in a manner that was more Oriental than Occidental, with all the virtues and flaws the two approaches imply. Resembling a Japanese rock garden, Heredia's sonnets may represent the pinnacle of Parnassist achievement.

My translation of "The Flight of the Centaurs," though free, dares not deviate too much from the original. An undisciplined flight of fancy would draw me to the attention of the un-Parnassian Activities Committee, a fate to be avoided at any cost.

THE FLIGHT OF THE CENTAURS

Nostrils flare as the panicked creatures rear,
rider fused into mount. The lion's stench
launches a terror-stricken avalanche
on sunset's steep slopes. The centaurs appear

in headlong flight, precipitously run,
leaping into chasms they can't tackle.
Stretching to watch the grizzly spectacle
Pelion the Black's and Ossa's peaks look on.

At times, a centaur of the untamed herd
will halt and whirl as if something occurred
to him before his momentary freeze,

because in the dim moonlight's metal flow,
he glimpsed, spilling onto the plain below,
the terrifying shade of Hercules.

FUITE DE CENTAURES

Ils fuient, ivres de meurtre et de rébellion,
Vers le mont escarpé qui garde leur retraite;
La peur les précipite, ils sentent la mort prête
Et flairent dans la nuit une odeur de lion.

Ils franchissent, foulant l'hydre et le stellion,
Ravins, torrents, halliers, sans que rien les arrête;
Et déjà, sur le ciel, se dresse au loin la crête
De l'Ossa, de l'Olympe ou du noir Pélion.

Parfois, l'un des fuyards de la farouche harde
Se cabre brusquement, se retourne, regarde,
Et rejoint d'un seul bond le fraternel bétail;

Car il a vu la lune éblouissante et pleine
Allonger derrière eux, suprême épouvantail,
La gigantesque horreur de l'ombre Herculéenne.

A footnote: Heredia, a very French poet, is sometimes confused with his
cousin Heredia, a very Spanish poet. They were both born in Cuba, but José
María de Heredia y Giraud went to live and make his mark in France, while
José María de Heredia y Campuzano (1803–1839) died as Cuba's national
poet three years before his cousin was born.

Labé

LOUISE LABÉ DIED SOMEWHERE in the French countryside, perhaps of the plague, a decade or so after the publication of the slim volume that preserved her name for the next four-and-a-half centuries. *Oeuvres de Louize Labé Lionnoize* was published in 1555, in the Renaissance heyday of Lyon, when the French provincial capital rivaled Paris as the cultural centre. Labé's book contained twenty-three sonnets in French and one in Italian, plus three elegies and a prose meditation on love. That was all she wrote (as far as we know). The daughter of one prosperous artisan and the widow of another, she was probably in her early forties when she died.

Like Sappho's poems, though on the basis of less evidence, Labé's are said to celebrate lesbian love. (Sappho of Lesbos was indisputably a Lesbian, at least in a geographical sense; about Labé all we know that she had been handed from one French rope-maker about thirty to forty years older than herself (her father) to another (her husband), which may be enough to turn any young woman into a lesbian. Whether or not Labé, once she learned the ropes (as it were), sought solace from her own sex,

43

she did dedicate her little volume to a local noblewoman. Although this, in itself, is evidence of nothing, it transferred the poet from the brackish backwaters of literature to the foaming rapids of women's studies in some American universities. In a 2006 edition of the *Complete Poems of Louise Labé* (University of Chicago Press), the famous "Sonnet 24" begins: *Sisters, do not reproach me that I've felt —* etc.

Sisters?

Mind you, people in glass houses shouldn't throw stones. I have taken significant liberties with the "24th Sonnet" myself. So that readers can judge, Labé's original follows my English version.

24TH SONNET

Think no less of me, ladies, for falling
too fast too easily, or for my core-
shattering pain, for my appalling
luck to be snared, of all things, by Amor

who trumps all, if Latin tags be trusted;
or for the additional remorse
because my passion may have crested
after long nights of crying myself hoarse.

Curb your sharp tongues, for you're not immune:
Vulcan stands poised, one spark, and next you see
high flames burning you, helpless, to a cinder!

You'll be singing quite another tune
when, after being tempted less than me,
you're harrowed even more and fall down harder.

XXIV

Ne reprenez, Dames, si j'ai aimé,
Si j'ai senti mille torches ardentes,
Mille travaux, mille douleurs mordantes.
Si, en pleurant, j'ai mon temps consumé,

Las! que mon nom n'en soit par vous blamé.
Si j'ai failli, les peines sont présentes,
N'aigrissez point leurs pointes violentes:
Mais estimez qu'Amour, à point nommé,

Sans votre ardeur d'un Vulcain excuser,
Sans la beauté d'Adonis accuser,
Pourra, s'il veut, plus vous rendre amoureuses:

En ayant moins que moi d'occasion,
Et plus d'étrange et forte passion.
Et gardez-vous d'être plus malheureuses.

Cellini

BENVENUTO CELLINI (1500–1571) was not a nice man. A brawler and a pederast, he was frequently in hot water with both the authorities and his neighbours. The Italian painter-soldier had to be on the run even in Renaissance Europe — that is, in a place and period that were far more lenient than ours about his particular tastes, and far less efficient in enforcing such objections as they may have had to them — so it is a safe bet that in our society he would have spent most of his life in jail. But Cellini was a Renaissance man in his virtues as well as in his vices; and — since he excelled in art, music, and literature as much as in braggadocio, manslaughter, and child molestation — he spent much of his life in ducal palaces.

In Vienna, on my ritual visits to the Kunsthistorische Museum that houses many of the *objects d'art* Cellini made for the princes and prelates of Europe — his golden salt cellar, his gold medallion of Leda and the Swan — I have often looked in awe at the handiwork of the lecherous goldsmith. The sonnet in this collection, the preface to his notorious autobiography, is a free but fairly faithful translation.

SONNET AS PREFACE TO HIS AUTOBIOGRAPHY

I will render my tortured life on paper,
a humble act of gratitude to God,
who fashioned me from clay as my creator,
then let me fashion beauty from the mud.

> Questa mia Vita travagliata io scrivo
> per ringraziar lo Dio della natura
> che mi diè l'alma e poi ne ha 'uto cura,
> alte diverse 'mprese ho fatte e vivo.

My destiny turned kind: I graduated
from misery's slave to be glory's client
with fate to grant me, albeit belated,
a sharp mind; manly looks; strength of a giant.

> Quel mio crudel Destin, d'offes'ha privo
> vita, or, gloria e virtú piú che misura,
> grazia, valor, beltà, cotal figura
> che molti io passo, e chi mi passa arrivo.

My sweet times and hopes vanished, but who frets
over lost causes, spilt milk, late regrets?
Having explored the distant realms of Pluto

Sol mi duol grandemente or ch'io cognosco
quel caro tempo in vanità perduto:
nostri fragil pensier sen porta 'l vento.

I'll settle now in lands that gave me birth,
and finish, as I set out, Benvenuto,
beneath the flowers of my Tuscan earth.

Poi che 'l pentir non val, starò contento
salendo qual'io scesi il Benvenuto
nel fior di questo degno terren tosco.

Hugo

VICTOR MARIE HUGO IS a giant as well as a whipping-boy of French literature. Worshipping and putting him down in the same breath has long been a parlour game for the French literati. Jean Cocteau famously described him once as a madman who thought he was Victor Hugo. When asked who was the greatest French poet, André Gide is said to have replied, "Victor Hugo, alas!"

"*Boöz endormi*," which Hugo published in 1859, is one of his most celebrated poems. It inspired my "Terzinas to Old Age," albeit in a backhanded sort of way. Hugo's sleeping Boaz and contemplative Ruth elegize and panegyrize the "eternal summer," the "golden sickle" of the late harvest, the sturdy ripeness of old age, whereas my "voice" and "chorus" lament age's feebleness and decrepitude. It would be possible to describe "voice" in "Terzinas to Old Age" as the counter-Boaz and "chorus" as the counter-Ruth. Needless to say, such a poetic dispute is also a form of homage.

There are no similarities in form, tone, or imagery between the two poems. There is no attempt at parody, no setting apart by imitation, and not even a superficial resemblance. Hugo's Boaz sleeps through twenty-two majestic quatrains; my counter-Boaz kvetches through six terzinas.

Age itself may account for some of the reasons for which age appears to Hugo in a different light: the prolific author of *Les Miserables*, born in 1802, wrote his ode to the potency of older males when he was still a mere pup, in his late fifties (he lived to be eighty-two). My modest attempt at counterpoint, composed at the age of seventy, while not nearly as majestic, might suffer from fewer illusions.

TERZINAS TO OLD AGE

A Voice:

I am December who used to be May.
Breezes and bloom then; now frost and decay.
Yesterday: tomorrow. Today: yesterday

Chorus:

Behold this timid soul who in his day used to be bold.
In times past, shining brass, reduced to rust, mildew and mould.
As Phoebus rose, he blossomed. As Phoebus sinks, he'll fold.

A Voice:

Younger than young at dawn, at dusk older than old.
Gold hair white after silver. White teeth black after gold.
A past — warm to the touch still; a future — cold.

Chorus:

Almost sagacious yesterday, today he's merely meek.
His knees buckle, the backbone bends, porous organs leak.
He whispers these stanzas, a voice too frail to speak.

A Voice:

I was like unto verdure once, am now like unto snow.
I used to wonder, waking up; near sleep, I nearly know.
Recently I came. I'm here. In no time I will go.

Chorus:

The body still of flesh and blood, the soul has turned to clay.
His days have vanished — vanished! — where to, no one can say.
Once flame, now ember. Call him December. He used to be May.

"Orpheus" is simply a free translation of one of my favorite poems. It strays from the original quite a bit but not because I thought I could improve on Hugo's verse: I just could not match it.

ORPHEUS

Listen to me, Uranus, the constructor:
I worship a girl. She's a sacred factor
in my life. Hear me, do not impede her,
azure-haired monster, Poseidon — I need her.
Attest, illustrious haven, Tanais,
you of dark waters and six-fingered bays,
and Zeus, whose divine favour disburses
the great cart of the night and Nyx's horses:
Witness, past giants; affirm, creatures new,
all-devouring Pluto blue of icy hue:
allow the wind of meadowlands to see
that I adore my sweet Eurydice
forever, everywhere. And if I fail
let heaven descend on me with hail,
till mangled with the wheat and fruit, I fall.
Do not put an occult mark on the wall.

ORPHEE

J'atteste Tanaïs, le noir fleuve aux six urnes
Et Zeus qui fait traîner sur les grands chars nocturnes
Rhéa par des taureaux et Nyx par des chevaux,
Et les anciens géants et les hommes nouveaux,
Pluton qui nous dévore, Uranus qui nous crée,
Que j'adore une femme et qu'elle m'est sacrée.
Le monstre aux cheveux bleus, Poséidon, m'entend ;
Qu'il m'exauce. Je suis l'âme humaine chantant,
Et j'aime. L'ombre immense est pleine de nuées,
La large pluie abonde aux feuilles remuées,
Borée émeut les bois, Zéphir émeut les blés.
Ainsi nos coeurs profonds sont par l'amour troublés.
J'aimerai cette femme appelée Eurydice,
Toujours, partout! Sinon que le ciel me maudisse,
Et maudisse la fleur naissante et l'épi mûr !
Ne tracez pas de mots magiques sur le mur.

Al-Ma'ari

CALLING ABUL ALA'A AL-MA'ARI (973–1057) Miltonesque would be a misnomer in reference to his poetry, but accurate with reference to his eyesight. The classic Arab poet resembled the classic English one in his paucity of outer and clarity of inner vision, though in other respects they were entirely different, in outlook as well as in style. The Western poet al-Ma'ari does resemble, in thematic interests, is Dante Alighieri. His *Risalat ul Ghufran* describes a visit to Paradise, where the Syrian poet's friends seem much happier than the Italian poet's enemies in Hell — but then al-Ma'ari may have been a kinder human being than Dante.

The author of *Risalat ul Ghufran* certainly spent much less time trying to secure patrons than the author of *The Divine Comedy*, even though he lived in a culture where patronage was just as important. The games of sycophancy fourteenth-century poets had to play in Ravenna or Florence were remarkably similar to games of sycophancy eleventh-century poets had to play in Baghdad or Tripoli, and Dante was better at them than al-Ma'ari. In consequence, the great Italian ate a richer diet and died significantly younger (at fifty-six) than his Arab counterpart (at eighty-four).

The book of al-Ma'ari's "paragraphs and periods" (*Al Fusul wal ghayat*), from which the poem in this collection is taken, characteristically describes itself by form rather than content, resembling al-Ma'ari's earlier "*Luzumiyat*" ("Necessities") that referred to the poems' elaborate rhyme schemes. Readers of Arabic call al-Ma'ari a virtuoso; it would explain his preoccupation with form. It is possible that he came up with such a reserved, technical title mainly to divert attention from people calling his inspired couplets a mockery of the Qur'an. I do not read Arabic, so I based my English version on George Faludy's Hungarian translation. I expect the great Arab poet would still recognize it, but perhaps only barely.

FROM THE BOOK OF PARAGRAPHS

Burning stakes blossom from the footsteps of Redeemers;
the Koran fashions daggers carried by true believers;
the atheist has faith in what his eyes reveal,
the Sufi, in what he sees with eyelids sealed.
It is a Buddhist doctrine that all doctrines must fail;
the Hebrew knows nothing, in exquisite detail;
the Brahmin fears risks that in his next life he runs;
the hedonist trembles, for his life comes only once
and briefly.
      In the great insane asylum
of this revolving earth, chaos creates the rules.
There are believing and unbelieving fools.

D'Annunzio

GABRIELE D'ANNUNZIO WAS BORN in a picturesque part of Europe, lived during a picturesque period of Italian history (1863–1938), and led a suitably picturesque life. He dabbled in various art forms — poetry, fiction, stage, film — and although today's reader might conclude that he excelled in none, he achieved respectable crafts-manship in all. His popularity as a writer was enhanced by his colourful life as a daredevil and a war hero. While he may have been admired by his contemporaries beyond his merits, his easy dismissal by posterity has been, I believe, equally baseless — or, rather, politically based.

Commissioned as a flight lieutenant in the Great War, d'Annunzio lost his right eye during a crash landing in 1916, but returned to active duty eight months later, in time to see action at Veliki, Faiti, and Isonzo. In these largely forgotten battles of the Great War the fifty-three-year-old poet-pilot was decorated and promoted to the rank of captain. By then his major works — including the collection *Poema paraisiaco* (1893), the novel *Le virgini delle rocce* (1895), and the tragedy *Francesca da Rimini* (1902) — were well behind him. His literary reputation made, d'Annunzio could concentrate on tearing it to shreds after the war by becoming Benito Mussolini's precursor, mentor, and later rival, in the early fascist movement. As his first move in 1919, the flamboyant poet and his followers seized the port city of Fiume (Rijeka) and declared war on the Italian royal state. (The war did not last long.)

There was something about the tragic theatricality of the corporatist, expansionary state, with its leader-cult and hero-worship, that appealed to some artists and intellectuals. D'Annunzio was certainly not alone; others included such luminous figures as Norway's Knut Hamsun and America's Ezra Pound. It should also be noted that d'Annunzio adamantly opposed Mussolini's alliance with Hitler, at some cost, and even danger, to himself. Mussolini, who had a way with metaphors, likened the poet to a rotten tooth in fascism's upper jaw that needed pulling or continual filling with gold. It was a toss-up, according to Il Duce, but in the end he chose filling up d'Annunzio, nicknamed Il Duce Primo, with gold.

In this collection, instead of trying to translate or paraphrase one of "the First Duce's" poems, I tried imagining a poem that d'Annunzio, an enthusiastic supporter of Italy's Ethiopian adventure, might have composed about the fiery Italian journalist Oriana Fallaci (1929–2006) if he had lived long enough to witness her battle to preserve Italy from encroaching "Eurabia." I make no attempt to assume d'Annunzio's voice or borrow his imagery, and offer only his likely take on Fallaci.

FALLACI IN MILAN

In this sixth year of the new millennium,
considering each measurement that matters,
the West seems in the pink; the East, in tatters.

Marx and Mao dethroned. It's rags, not riches
for ex-serfs of the great man of steel, Stalin,
whose successors excel mainly in stealing.

Self-immolating Islam curses and twitches
in its own blood, not yet having the skill
to draw much blood from others — though it's learning.

Despite the goodwill, wealth, personal valour
of some rulers, and oil in the ground,
the Levant languishes in Biblical squalour.

Time marches. The logic of the migrant
follows a path from famine to feast,
from stagnation to a life that's vibrant,
to the free West from the despotic East.

Measuring ages by a rule of thumb,
as history's relentless wheel keeps turning,
a cycle starts, a clock begins to tick,
the lean grow sensitive, the satiated numb,

the mean protest, the good don't give a damn,
and London fiddles while London's burning.

A cricket chorus of the Left that frets
unceasingly about nuclear threats
goes on to view with exquisite aplomb
the Muslim population bomb.
The word is imprecise: there's no explosion,
at least not literally, from the Islamic womb,
the process throughout Europe is erosion.
A puzzled population, getting older,
feebly looks on as Mesopotamia,
seeps through the soil, the air, the blood,
a trickle yesterday, today a flood,
mixes with Tunis, Algeria,
till those who go to sleep in France or Spain,
wake in Eurabia.

Europe having been peeled of her defenses,
a big white onion, layer by layer,
the old alarm: *Italia irredenta*!
appears warranted as a muezzin calls
the prophet's vanguard camped inside the walls,
the faithful of Roma, to evening prayer.
Across the drawbridge infiltrators saunter,
with no Tancred to relieve the siege,

and only one Cassandra-clone, a sage
fool, rails by the gaping gates, to counter
rabid Arab with gilt Florentine rage.
Behind the walls huddle the moribund,
across the moat come surging the fecund.
One woman only, in white, a chic crusader,
makes a last stand for the western realm
in Rizzoli's mall between Duomo and La Scala
against a tide from the Gulf States to Ghana,
wielding a quill-shaped cudgel... Good luck, Oriana!

Villon

GEORGE ORWELL'S OBSERVATION ABOUT the Spanish surrealist painter Salvador Dalí — "one ought to be able to hold in one's head simultaneously the two facts that Dalí is a good draughtsman and a disgusting human being. The one does not invalidate or, in a sense, affect the other" — applies equally to a fifteenth-century drifter named François Villon. An exceptionally gifted lyricist and balladeer, Villon was by his own credible admission also a thief and a killer.

Born around 1431, known to some as François de Montcorbier or François Des Loges, Villon's life illustrates the amorality of talent. Raised by an uncle, a kindly cleric, the precocious young scholar turns bad. In today's terms, he drops out, joins a gang, gets into trouble with the law. After periods of banishment from Paris, having robbed, pimped, brawled, and copulated his way through late-medieval France, the thirty-two-year-old vagrant disappears from history. January 5, 1463, the date of a commutation of his death sentence by hanging to a new term of banishment, is the last entry in the official record. After that, Villon vanishes. The likelihood of his having lived to a ripe old age is not great. "*Mais ou sont les neiges d'antan?"* as he wrote, in a different context. "But where are the snows of yesteryear?" (English by Dante Gabriel Rosetti, whose nineteenth-century translation has not yet been surpassed.)

Was this disorderly derelict the greatest poet of France, as some claim? Possibly — but poetry not being a horse race, this is a question we need not answer.

In Villon's magnum opus, *Le grand testament,* the violent vagabond remonstrates with others for not having enough of various qualities he himself so conspicuously lacks, from altruism to patience, from restraint to charity. Utterly sincere, the poet sounds the way he probably was: impulsive, self-centred, self-pitying, self-romanticising — an immature twit, possibly with attention deficit disorder. Yet stanza after stanza he sets out his true self with a convincing, unconventional, easy grace that makes the reader both savour and devour his words.

Talent, an enviable commodity, is often poured into unworthy vessels. Konstantin Sergeyevich Stanislavsky, the father of "method" acting (1863–1938), admonished performers that they should admire art in themselves, not themselves in art — but it is not so easy to tell where one ends and the other begins. Would Villon the poet have still existed with Villon the bandit surgically removed from his soul? Or were the two inextricably intertwined?

Orwell wanted to stress that an artist's gifts and skills should not blind us to his moral flaws, just as his moral flaws should not make us deny his artistic gifts and skills. Desirable as this undoubtedly is, it leaves the door open for admiring an artist for the wrong reasons. An amoral celebration of talent can turn into a celebration of talented immorality.

Whether or not the greatest French lyric poet of all times, Villon was unknown in his own. He was discovered in the sixteenth century by Clément Marot (1496–1544), a court poet and royal librarian, quite popular himself in his day. After a period near the top of the charts, Villon slipped back in the literary ratings game, until re-descovered in the twentieth century, this time for his vices as much as for his virtues. Stalin-worshipping Bertolt Brecht (1898–1956), front-runner in last century's Villon-revival, made his *Threepenny Opera*'s Marxist Mackie Messer, or Mack the Knife, a hero, not in spite of his Villonesque banditry, but because of it. Kicking "bourgeois morality" in the teeth was part of George Faludy's agenda as well when he introduced his irresistible Faludy-Villon to the reading public in 1938, even though he detested Stalin. It seems to me that appreciating Villon requires not only tolerance for sinners, but also some tolerance for sin.

I confess: I do appreciate Villon. Some of it is nostalgia; it was Villon-via-Faludy that drew aside the curtain for me on the world of rhyming reasons that I believe poetry to be. But some of it is the mature judgement of a septuenegerian who has read a lot of poetry and has learned to separate, as they say, the brain from the kidney.

Having a strong adolescent streak, Villon is most rewarding to read in adolescence. To an extent this may be true of all poets, but it applies to some more than to others. It especially does to the author of *The Great Testament*. Owing to a high testosterone content, his poetry might even have a special resonance for boys — it certainly did for me.*

In this collection, two poems — "Poet on the Gallows" and

"Pierre the Red Coquillard" — are exercises I've written on Villon's themes in the French poet's manner with faint echoes of Faludy, while "Danse Macabre" is my free translation of Faludy, with strong echoes of Villon.

DANSE MACABRE

The Emperor held court. In his hair
seven stars made a diadem,
the Big Dipper turned in his navel,
kneeling slaves paid homage to him.
On his bronzed arm the disc of the new moon
cast a silver sickle of light.
Only a humble clown sat meekly
by the Emperor's throne and cried.
"Why are you crying," he roared, "my sword
touches every man's heart; I trust
by now I own the earth …" That night, a skeleton
blew him away like a speck of dust.
— We played the tyrant, one and all,
years flew like minutes to amaze us,
by the spilt dewdrops of your blood
be merciful to us, Prince Jesus.

At his gothic window the Doctor wailed:
"Lord, on which one of these hills
is your magic nectar growing
that is said to cure all ills?"
And through the door an emaciated don
danced across the den with a stein
in segmented fingers of bone
offering colourless wine:
"Drink, this grape is euphorically cool,
dries every wound, makes all pain numb,
drink up, colleague, from this deep chalice
only the first drop stings your tongue."
— We were false experts, one and all,
years flew like minutes to amaze us,
by the spilt dewdrops of your blood
be merciful to us, Prince Jesus.

The Child stood at the rim of the well
in a torn shirt and a pair of clay-
coloured slippers, and looked at his own
face in the water that called him to play.
"… The moon-maiden will give you candy
by the bucketful if you come
and we'll play tag with the bullfrogs
in the light of the rising sun."

"I'm coming!" he said, and the water of the well
reared tadpoles on his swelling belly, while
smug Death offered his mother as a gift
the clay-coloured slippers with a slimy smile.
— We played childish games, one and all,
years flew like minutes to amaze us,
by the spilt dewdrops of your blood
be merciful to us, Prince Jesus.

At her cracked mirror sat the Harlot:
"The flood of my hair's still red, so why
is it that no lovers, companions
call me, and old friends pass me by?
The lips of my lap are readily parted,
my nipples are hard as diamonds still …"
when Jawbone, the slickest pimp, hailed her
stepping across the window sill:
"Hop to it, Ho', you dance with me,
your ancient johns have gone to ruin,
let larvae spread their wedding feast
on the wilted purple of your groin."
— We twisted in lust, one and all,
years flew like minutes to amaze us,
by the spilt dewdrops of your blood
be merciful to us, Prince Jesus.

Pitch-black midnight embraced the rooftops,
an owl's scream pierced the misty cold,
the Banker out on his journey
to bury deep his bloodstained gold.
Seven devils hiding behind Death
stood at the crossroads. Intrepid,
the Banker drew his sword. The skeleton
whispered to him: "You see, stupid,
you're still clutching your moneybag,
this iron spike gives you a clout,
and you get buried, not your gold,
and who will ever dig you out?"
— We were grim peddlers, one and all,
years flew like minutes to amaze us,
by the spilt dewdrops of your blood
be merciful to us, Prince Jesus.

The Lady sat in her silk boudoir
and shrieked in terror: "Too soon, too soon!"
But he had already embraced the fair
domes of her hips in his arms of doom.
"Let me have one more languid kiss,
one more dress of pearls, one more vain,
easy, casual compliment,
or only one more night of pain …"

But painting a circular stain on her breast
that grew, as cancer grows, lumpy and rough,
he hoisted her white body on his back
and carried and carried and carried her off.
— We were parasites, one and all,
years flew like minutes to amaze us,
by the spilt dewdrops of your blood
be merciful to us, Prince Jesus.

The Alchemist stood by his fire
and looked at the sands that had run out.
"God or Satan, give me one more day,
my retorts are brimming at the mouth;
the great puzzle is hiding inside
the white flames of my kilns of clay:
just one more day will see it yielding,
I'll have it solved in one more day!"
"This riddle?" asked a voice. "You will not."
And held him firmly, while the test-
tubes blew up, with icy hands.
"You'll go to sleep now, like the rest."
— We looked for answers, one and all,
years flew like minutes to amaze us,
by the spilt dewdrops of your blood
be merciful to us, Prince Jesus.

The bells of pestilence rang in the plague
in front of the cathedral of Rheims,
and on a bubonic Easter Sunday
it shook the stout Bishop by the hands:
"I did compose this tune for you,
let's go, my lord! I ring my bells.
Be pope or prophet, priest or scholar
who in the holy script excels,
be bishop or a heretic, whose
sole relics are his blackened bones;
say Mass below: I peel my laughter
from the chill belfries of the domes."
— We were hypocrites, one and all,
years flew like minutes to amaze us,
by the spilt dewdrops of your blood
be merciful to us, Prince Jesus.

The old Peasant stood in the barnyard
at nightfall; he expected him.
"My worn body, it fetches no price,
give it away, Death. Let's begin,
brother reaper: our land is poor
and nothing will increase the yield.
Take this body, it's good manure,
and dress it deep into the field."
He nodded, then carried him slowly,

and sowed him, sowed him, sowed him in
like farmers sowing in the new seed
or poppies blowing in the wind …
— We go underground, one and all,
years fly like minutes to amaze us,
by the spilt dewdrops of your blood
be merciful to us, Prince Jesus.

"Danse Macabre" is a Faludy-Villon ballad called "*Haláltánc ballada*" in the original. My version is a reasonably faithful translation. The poet himself (Faludy, of course, not Villon) proofread an earlier draft, published in John Robert Colombo's anthology, *Two For Faludy*. My own Villon-variations, "Poet on the Gallows" and "Pierre the Red Coquillard," are poems written in homage to Faludy's Villon-variations.

POET ON THE GALLOWS

Dawn stabs a bloody finger at the Seine,
Gawk and shiver, my fellow citizen.
A swig will take the chill off your pelvis:
Villon, François, poet, at your service!

As my life reaches its apogee
I offer for it no apology.
Some cobble cloying sonnets in an arbour,
I'll perform instead my danse macabre.

Familiar with hunger and with thirst
I flattered many princes, killed a priest.
At the gates of hell I will not stand alone
As the Fiend divides us, each soul to his own.

I am a Frenchman, born of the elite,
At a moment no moment shall surpass.
Paris, my city, is spread beneath my feet,
My slender neck supports a weighty ass.

PIERRE THE RED COQUILLARD

His ancient hat tilted over one ear,
a dagger sitting cross-eyed in his belt,
at times a mite unsteady on his feet
(damned spirits, they will do this to a man),
a bandit, who could lead cops by the nose,
and keep the magistrates awake at night;
be everywhere and not be anywhere,
this was Pierre, the prostitutes' delight.

He liked to dress his working girls in white
and when he had a coin or two to spare
he'd take his favorite, Margot, to pose
in ribbons he had bought her in the square.
He was the prince of pimps, Pierre the Red,
a man to charm the lock off any door,
lay, on the altar, a blushing newlywed,
ambush the rich, do no harm to the poor.

Meat, music, grog, fat Margot's derriere,
that was the life, and let no one mock it.
He painted Paris pink, pimping Pierre:
a pockmarked face and a well-lined pocket.
We loved him. Why trade easy laughter
for whatever is supposed to come after
the music stops, smiles freeze, and a hush
falls over streets from which all souls vanish?

Never! We sucked the last drop worth imbibing,
filled our bellies and dropped our pants,
and afterwards swore on a stack of bibles
he was a brigand to eclipse all brigands.
But this proved to be too much for the hangman
who sat quietly polishing his hate,
and said to Pierre: "My vultures and I
expect you for a meal. Please don't be late."

The newlywed's challenge, Margot's delight,
the pockmarked villain with the tilted hat,
who liked to promenade local hookers,
deprive magistrates of their sleep at night
and lead the cops of Paris by the nose
for the amusement of the onlookers —
one morning, with nothing better to do,
made up his mind to keep the rendezvous.

And so it happened that Pierre the Red
was staring at the gallows by the Seine.
He may have felt some moisture irrigating
his eyes (damned spirits!) but, because by then
earthly matters were well beyond debating,
he removed the old hat from his head
and mounted the scaffold with steady steps.
It's bad manners to keep the hangman waiting.

* My 72-year-old self can still hear, even if no longer with the clarity of my 16-year-old ghost, a stanza from Villon's *"Chanson to the Beauties of Paris"*:

"De tres beau parler tiennent chaires,
Ce dit-on, les Napolitaines,
Et que sont bonnes cacquetoeres
Allemanses et Bruciennes;
Soient Grecques, Egyptiennes,
De Hongrie ou d'autre pays,
Espaignolles ou Castellannes,
Il n'est bon bec que de Paris ..."

Address yourself to any creature
on this continent or overseas
of familiar or foreign feature
European or Singhalese;
seek Berber barbarians for attraction,
 flaming Flemings to teach you kiss:
it's piffle. Wait till you see in action
the magic maidens of Paris.

(translation: Jonas at sixteen)

Heine

IN ADDITION TO BEING one of the great poets of his era, Heinrich Heine (1797–1856) has remained one of its great cult figures. Like Freemasonry's secret symbols or gestures, snippets of Heine's poems link people of ethno-cultural affinity. Such signs are capable of establishing instant kinship. In the 1980s, when I encountered the Vienna-born (but Oxford-accented) British publisher, George Weidenfeld, in a Toronto restaurant, within minutes we found ourselves ritually exchanging lines of Heine in lieu of letters of accreditation. *"Und der Sklave sprach,"* I recall offering, to which Lord Weidenfeld instantly replied, *"ich heiße Mohamet, ich bin aus Yemmen."* After this, with our bona fides established, we could continue the conversation as if we had known each other all our lives.

Before saying anything more about Heine, I cannot resist inserting here "The Asra" by which Lord Weidenfeld and I recognized each other's tribal affiliation. This is for readers who understand German, obviously, but also for people who like glancing at passages in languages they do not understand. (I cannot be the only one.) Others can skip to the next page.

Täglich ging die wunderschöne
Sultanstochter auf und nieder
Um die Abendzeit am Springbrunn,
Wo die weißen Wasser plätschern.

Täglich stand der junge Sklave
Um die Abendzeit am Springbrunn,
Wo die weißen Wasser plätschern;
Täglich ward er bleich und bleicher.

Eines Abends trat die Fürstin
Auf ihn zu mit raschen Worten:
Deinen Namen will ich wissen,
Deine Heimat, deine Sippschaft!

Und der Sklave sprach: Ich heiße
Mohamet, ich bin aus Yemmen,
Und mein Stamm sind jene Asra,
Welche sterben wenn sie lieben.

THE ASRA

Daily did the Sultan's fabled
Headstrong beauty of a daughter
Pass the fountain as the sun set
Where the green waters meander.

Daily did a young slave wander
By the fountain as the sun set
Where the green waters meander
Pale, and fast becoming paler.

One day, lest her bold thoughts fail her,
The Sultan-child hailed him rashly:
"Let me know your name, relations,
Your birth-land and tribal kinship."

Spoke the slave: "I am Mohammed,
Yemen, my birthplace, is nearby.
I come from that tribe of Asra
Who, when they fall in love, die."

Heine was born in Düsseldorf, Germany, to upper-middle-class Jewish parents, but purchased what he called his "ticket of admission into European culture" in 1825 by converting from Judaism to Christianity. He followed his first cross-cultural adventure by a second one six years later, when he left Germany for France, never to return, except for a short visit in 1843. Bedridden for the last eight years of his life, he died in what he described as a "mattress-grave" in Paris at the age of fifty-nine.

The second cultural crossing was more traumatic for a poet working — and working wonders — specifically in the German language. Heine never quite got over it. During his exile he continued writing in German about German themes and subjects, though not exclusively. His poetry and polemical writing range from the lyrical to the satirical, one mood often, and memorably, informing the other. Describing the author of *"Du bist wie eine Blume"* as a mixture of Leonard Cohen and Thomas Paine would be too facile, but not altogether wrong. No German poet has been put to music more often (or by better composers) — not even Goethe or Nikolaus Lenau, the most melancholy of the *Sturm und Drang* troubadours (1802–1850). As for Heine's remark about Germany, "they begin by burning books, and will end up by burning people," few observations have proven more prophetic.

In this collection I offer two more free (read: capricious) adaptations of Heine ("Pine, Dreaming" and "From 'Lazarus'") and a two-part poem, "In Homage," the last one being what its title implies.

PINE, DREAMING

In northern lands a lonely pine
    atop a precipice
drifts off to sleep behind a steep
    incline of glassy ice.

His dream is of a distant palm
    mourning among the crude
desert rocks of her native East
    in sun-drenched solitude.

FROM "LAZARUS"

Never mind your empty symbols,
parables, priests, holy vermin.
The damn question needs an answer,
not a pussyfooting sermon.

While the good must drag their crosses,
bleeding, thorn-torn — how can ugly,
wicked victors on high horses
ride by so easily and smugly?

Whose fault is it? Is our good Lord
a smidgeon less than almighty?
Or is he himself mocking justice?
No way would he do that ... Or might he?

So we keep asking the question
till decrepitude or cancer
stops us with a mouthful of dirt --
But would you call that an answer?

IN HOMAGE

1.

When Caesar crossed the Rubicon
not knowing if his luck would last
he used a gambler's metaphor:
"The die is cast."

Antiquity had forty-nine
years to go yet, after a scorn-
ful Caesar came, saw, conquered.
Then Christ was born.

Tempted, scourged, nailed to the cross
for sowing salvation's discord,
he said, in words as clear as air:
"Forgive them, Lord."

When soldiers rolled dice for his robe
heaven's sun spun into eclipse.
Man's son suffered the vinegar-soaked
sponge touch his lips.

Rome crumbled. Years marched like legions.
The earth orbited, as it must.
God raised Christ to his right and rendered
Caesar to dust.

2.

As the ponderous universe revolves
one wonders: is it all a Judas kiss?
God poses puzzles that he never solves.
Is each new dawn a yawn? Each height
  a new abyss?

With mankind standing on the brink
of novel closures and erasures,
catastrophes are simmering.
Christ's mystery quickens the pulse.
  So does Caesar's.

Who renders what to whom and in which order?
Does Conscience trump King, or is King the test?
Is the right word explosive? Exquisite?
Eli, Eli, lama sabachtani? Or is it:
  Alea jacta est?

Nietzsche

OH, NIETZSCHE, FRIEDRICH WILHELM, the softest heart to promulgate the harshest philosophy, and crack under the strain by the age of forty-five! Nietzsche, author of *The Will to Power*, creator of the *Übermensch* or Superman, the creature imagining himself *Beyond Good and Evil*, who after announcing the death of God appropriated for himself the voice of Zarathustra, thereby essentially replacing the deity; Nietzsche, the poet, aphorist, and philosophy professor who revolutionized ethical thinking in the West and whose last conscious act before collapsing into insanity, mental and physical, was said to have been to protect a draft horse from being beaten.

This final story, possibly apocryphal, has the philosopher making a public spectacle of himself in the Italian town of Turin, trying to prevent a coachman from whipping his horse by cradling the animal's head in his arms. By then, in 1889, Nietzsche had completed all his major work. Having exhausted and severed virtually all his literary and philosophical relationships, he still had ten years of life to look forward to as a barking mad recluse in the home of his mother and sister.

Friedrich Nietzsche (1844–1900) was a precocious scholar, attaining full professorship by the age of twenty-four at the University of Basel. The Prussian-born thinker had been influenced by such seminal figures of European thought as the German and Danish philosophers Arthur Schopenhauer (1788–1860) and Søren Kierkegaard (1813–1855). He in turn, during the next twenty years, came to influence such stellar representatives of Western civilization as Richard Wagner (1813–1883), Fyodor Dostoyevsky (1821–1881), the Swiss-German historian Jacob Burckhardt (1818–1897), August Strindberg (1849–1912), the Danish-Jewish scholar Georg Brandes (1842–1927), the Swiss-German poet Carl Spitteler (1845–1924), and the Swiss-German author Gottfried Keller (1819–1890) — to offer just a short sample. Less happily, Nietzsche's influence continued well beyond twenty years, until it was embraced by a young Austrian house painter named Adolf Hitler (1889–1945).

Nietzsche and Hitler created an explosive mix, which is not my purpose to explore here. One can easily see the dangers of a Viennese flophouse inmate like young Hitler fancying himself a *Superman*, belonging to a *master race*, possessing the *Will to Power*, shedding the *slave morality* of an enfeebled Judeo-Christian ethic, taking the place of a *dead God*, and when *going to woman*, like *Zarathustra*, not forgetting his *whip*. Ideas have consequences, one of them being that semi-literate morons may read them. Then, of course, they may interpret them literally, swallow them whole, spew them out undigested, and act upon them idiotically one way or another. Presumably that was why, after the incident involving the Tree of Knowledge, God considered it wiser to shut down operations in the Garden of Eden.

Nietzsche's compassionate side proved not to be "beyond good and evil." In the end it defeated the "blond beast" in his soul — true, at the cost of his sanity. When it came to choose in Turin (if the anecdote is true) the author of *Thus Spake Zarathustra* sided with the beaten horse, not the whip hand of the master race.

My sole variation on a theme by Nietzsche in this book is "Abandoned," a lyric lament of the poet in horse-hugging mood, freely translated and fused with the rhythms of a folk song. In music, I'm not fond of the genre known as "fusion" — say, between classical and jazz — but this poem is one of my favorites.

ABANDONED

Late in the fall
through fields of clay
the muddy streams
sluggishly flow.
Low-flying crows
smelling decay
with weary screams
circle the town.
Soon it will snow.

Willows recall
daylight's delight,
the grass was tall
the sunshine white.
Now clouds are low
and skies are dark,
the crying crows
perch in the park.
Soon it will snow.

He who can call
a home his own
such dismal day,
well is the soul.
He can look on
as crows depart
with plaintive cries,
then wrap in ice
his bleeding heart.

Doomed is the soul
of one who has no
home of his own.
As crying crows
circle the town
and people shut
door after door,
he shall look on
and say no more.

Soon it will snow.

Magister Martinus

MARTINUS OF BIBERACH WAS a theologian from Heilbronn, Germany. He composed the following four lines as his epitaph:

> Ich leb, waiss nit wie lang,
> Ich stirb und waiss nit wann,
> Ich fahr, waiss nit wohin,
> Mich wundert, dass ich froehlich bin.

The lines were duly inscribed on his gravestone when he passed away in 1498, and have been anthologized to the hilt ever since. No wonder, because they score a bulls-eye. As far as we know, that is all he wrote.

EPITAPH

I live. For how long, I don't know,
can't tell the day I'm due to go,
or where I'm going when I die.
I feel cheerful. I wonder why.

Kürenberger, The

"DER KÜRENBERGER" WAS A knight-troubadour or *Minnesinger* roaming the twelfth-century hills of lower Austria. Also known as Der von Kürenberg, he probably pursued his craft in the region of present-day Linz. Such musical knight-errants would usually go from stronghold to stronghold on the strengths of a combination of their romantic errands and singing engagements, doing some falconry, hunting, and carousing between gigs. "The Falcon Song," written in a form known variously as the Niebelung-strophe or the Kürenberg-strophe, is one of the best-known examples of the genre. I translated it with gusto, taking considerable liberties:

THE FALCON SONG

Hand-raised myself a falcon bird,
by year's end she was grown.
Tenderly tamed her, but she still
seemed restless, prone to roam.

Gilded her feathers carefully
especially her wing,
one day she wheeled and flew away,
snapping her silver string.

At dusk today or just before,
I saw a falcon bird.
Trailing behind, a silver string,
she wouldn't heed my word.
Gold shimmered underneath her wing
in answer to my calls.
May merciful God help restore
all disunited souls.

The *Minnesinger* knight-troubadours did perhaps tilt at wind-mills with abandon, but they took their poetry seriously. English speakers may find the medieval German not too onerous to decipher:

Ich zôch mir einen valken mêre danne ein jâr.

dô ich in gezamete als ich in wolte hân

und ich im sîn gevidere mit golde wol bewant,

er huop sich ûf vil hôhe und floug in anderiu lant.

Sît sach ich den valken schône fliegen:

er fuorte an sînem fuoze sîdine riemen,

und was im sîn gevidere alrôt guldîn.

got sende si zesamene die gerne geliep wellen sîn!

In the second poem, I took all manner of liberties, making "Unlit Stars" a variation on the troubadour's theme. In my version the unlit or virgin stars in the constellation of Canis Major were added, along with twelve additional lines, to Der von Kürenberg's eight-line "*Dieser Stern im Dunkeln,*" best known in modern times for Kurt Weill having put it to music. (*Frauentanz,* op. 10)

UNLIT STAR

Carinthia's skies are dark as blight,
your eyes, like virtue, bright.
When virgin stars rise in the night,
they hide their light.

Be like an unlit star, demure,
sit at your window, mute.
Respond not to your troubadour
strumming his lute.

When called to supper, murmur grace,
sip wine under duress.
Unlit stars move without a trace.
No guest shall guess

a lady lithe, remote and fleet,
eyes downcast, all in white,
may soon be on her way to meet
her errant knight.

At table, when I lift my stein,
finger the tulip in your hair,
and none shall easily divine
who, when, what, where.

It occurs to me that some people may not know Kurt Weill. It's their loss — though not as great a loss as devotees of *Die Dreigroschenoper* (Mack the Knife, etc.) would think. The German composer (1900–1950) defined himself as a "socialist" (read: communist) first and a musician second, but his music proved to have a longer shelf-life than his politics. He was addicted to the same type of ugly round spectacles as the playwright Bertolt Brecht, with whom he collaborated on *The Threepenny Opera* and other works. There was a time when all Marxist intellectuals seemed to wear hideous glasses for extreme myopia. My father thought they went well with their ideologies.

Lermontov

RUSSIA'S MILITARY MINNESINGER REMINDS me of "Der Kürenber-ger" in his ironic-romantic lyricism as well as in his handiness with both pen and sword. Being number two, Mikhail Yuryevich Lermontov (1814–1841) had to try harder, and he did. He was always just a smidgeon more Byronic than Aleksandr Pushkin. Not just more romantic, Lermontov was perhaps even more patriotic than his idol, and died in an even sillier duel at an even earlier age. Pushkin was thirty-seven when Georges d'Anthes shot him in 1837; when Nikolai Martinov felled Lermontov four years later, the poet was not yet twenty-seven. D'Anthes was a social acquaintance who had flirted with Pushkin's wife; Martinov was a drinking buddy who had quarreled with his volatile friend.

Neither of Russia's great national poets was wholly Russian by ethnicity. Lermontov's foreign blood was a little more removed, coming from an early seventeenth-century Scottish ancestor named Learmount or Learmont who settled in Russia during Mikhail Feodorovich Romanov's reign. This was almost two generations before Pushkin's great-grandfather, a North African "blackamoor" named Ibrahim Petrovitch Gannibal, was gifted as a child to Czar Peter the Great.

Lermontov surpassed Pushkin — ever so slightly — in pugnacity and in playing the role of the poet as envisaged by the *Sturm und Drang* period of Wertherian romanticism. He fell behind, albeit not very far, in the sparkle and power of his poetry. He lagged considerably behind, though, in output: Pushkin's was prodigious and Lermontov's slim, even taking into account the ten extra years by which Pushkin managed to postpone having himself shot.

Both poems in this collection are free translations, not straying too far from Lermontov's somewhat prickly originals in either form or content. The first one is a splendid example of a power-and-penniless poet with an attitude.

GOOD-BYE

Let the critics of our friendship
— convention's footmen — roll their eyes.
Their low prejudices are wrenching,
sully your renommé as a wife,

but I won't genuflect to vested
proprieties at any price,
for right and wrong, however rusted,
my private judgement must suffice.

Like you, I prefer peace's pauses
to battle's catapults of stone.
Like you, I visit people's houses,
but reside entirely in my own.

At balls, I chat with fools and sages,
but listen only to my heart,
I live today, but for the ages,
I live here, but in a world apart.

We don't cheat so we won't be cheated.
We met; we say farewell again.
Our friendship wasn't much joy; at least let
our parting be without much pain.

Next, in Lermontov's sage advice to the Georgian maiden,
I suspect the "northern butterfly" is the poet himself. After all,
the dashing officer wasn't nicknamed "the poet of the Caucasus"
for nothing.

TO A GEORGIAN MAIDEN

Don't cry for him, my little star,
a waste of time, the lad is gone.
Erase him from your mind. There are
whole regiments of Georgian
fellows of form and fire to
delight in, who admire you.
Let them orbit around your sun.
Forget your pallid Russian.

He came into our quiet dale,
he saw, he conquered. It appears
he tried the nectar of your lips,
his words still echo in your ears …
One day this northern butterfly
flitted away. You weep, but why?
Where sweet smiles, tasty kisses fail,
can tears prevail?

By the way, readers may notice a resemblance between Lermontov's advice to the Georgian maiden and the advice Sir John Suckling (1609–1642) offered to an English youth, reproduced here, with which the Russian poet may have been familiar:

Why so pale and wan, fond lover?
Prithee, why so pale?
Will, when looking well can't move her,
Looking ill prevail?
Prithee, why so pale?
Why so dull and mute, young sinner?
Prithee, why so mute?
Will, when speaking well can't win her,
Saying nothing do 't?
Prithee, why so mute?

Quit, quit for shame! This will not move;
This cannot take her.
If of herself she will not love,
Nothing can make her.
The devil take her!

Hofmannstahl, von

CHANGING KEY. HUGO VON Hofmannstahl (1874–1929) was the great-grandson of a Jewish merchant, Isaak Löw Hofmann, raised to nobility by the Habsburg emperor Ferdinand I in 1835. A poet and all-around man of letters, he was a founding member of the Viennese avant garde, a sparkling generation brilliantly described in Stefan Zweig's 1941 memoir, *The World of Yesterday*. In today's world, Hofmannstahl is probably best remembered as the librettist of such operas as *Der Rosenkavalier* or *Ariadne auf Naxos*.

As the favorite collaborator of Nazi Germany's showpiece opera composer, Richard Strauss, he was also noted for the irony of being — *horribile dictu* — a Jew. So, by the way, was Strauss's second favorite librettist — Zweig. This was a source of ongoing friction between the Nazis, who had a taste for Strauss (1864–1949) and hated his taste in collaborators. The great maestro Strauss, Hermann Goering's personally appointed president of the Nazi State Bureau of Music, was neither anti- nor philo-Semitic: he just liked quality text and wanted to get along.

What warrants this short detour is that, for some contemporary historians, having been Strauss's Jew is Hofmannstahl's main claim to fame. I have found this far less interesting than his uniquely dark lyricism. For me, Hofmannstahl stands for the proposition that translating poetry from one language to another is so difficult as to be almost undesirable.

Hofmannstahl begins one of his poems with the line: "*Und Kinder wachsen auf mit tiefen Augen ...*" This line, simple, arresting, and evocative in German, has made "*Ballade des äußeren Lebens*" an instant anthology piece. Reading it in conjunction with the next two lines — "*Die von nichts wissen, wachsen auf und sterben, / Und alle Menschen gehen ihre Wege*" — elevates the stanza to a thing of considerable beauty. Try as one might, no variation of *"And children grow up with deep eyes / Who know nothing, grow up and die, / And all men go their way"* can come close to it. One has to switch, as I did in "The Ballad of External Existence," to something like "And children grow up, deep-eyed. They retire / looking vacant, then die. They are relying / on someone's say-so that they've gone the distance" before one has any hope of approaching poetry again, but by doing so, one must depart from Hofmannstahl's original. People going their way is not the same as people going the distance.

The solution, as far as I can see, is not to worry about anything extraneous to the task at hand, which is to write a poem in English. The most respectful response to being inspired by a German poem may be to put it quietly down and do nothing. The second most respectful, it seems to me, is to resist trying to shoehorn it into English. Best simply to write an English poem in homage to it, acknowledging the inspiration — which is what I tried to do with the poem of Strauss's librettist, the Austrian-Jewish nobleman.

THE BALLAD OF EXTERNAL EXISTENCE

And children grow up, deep-eyed. They retire
looking vacant, then die. They are relying
on someone's say-so that they've gone the distance.

And bitter seeds mature into beguiling
and tender fruit, to end up nightly lying
like dead birds under trees. With no resistance

out spills the empty wind that blows relentless
as words flow in and out of human faces,
as muscles alternately lust and slumber.

Look at a pointless highway that replaces
pastures with pavement, where passage leave no traces,
and comatose hamlets aridly encumber

living landscapes. Who built them all? And will
they never end? Is their fatal resemblance
to the real world a cautionary tale?

And why are we laughing, crying, turning pale?
Why do grown men seek solitude's relief
or cower hearing rolls of distant thunder?

What do we gain from seeing or believing?
Yet he who steps up to say simply: "Evening"
is uttering a peerless word of wonder,

a dense drop from a honeycomb of grief.

Hofmannstahl and his friends in Vienna and Berlin were all gifted people, bound by threads of art and modernity, and divided by fashions of race and politics. A near-equal mix of Jews and Gentiles, they included such men of letters, stage, and music as Jean (Johan) Sibelius, the Finnish composer (1865–1957); Max Reinhardt, the German stage director (1873–1943); Stefan George, the German symbolist poet (1868–1933); Peter Altenberg, the Viennese writer (1859–1919); and Arthur Schnitzler, the Austrian playwright (1862–1931). Their friend and collaborator, von Hofmannstahl lived a charmed life almost until the end. He even managed to die in time: imploding, like the stock market, in 1929, four years before Hitler came to power. He was unable to avoid the tragic fate of most poets, though: he died of a stroke two days after his son's suicide.

Laforgue

IT WOULD BE WRONG to suggest that Jules Laforgue (1860–1887) was the only French symbolist with a sense of humour, but one could suggest that he was in the minority. Whether this quality, relatively un-French and decidedly un-symbolist, was due to his having been born in Montevideo, Uruguay, where his expatriate father was a teacher, or to his being influenced by modern English-language poetry — carrying the infatuation far enough to actually marry an English girl named Leah Lee — would be hard to say. Many would dispute the premise, arguing that a) the French do have a sense of humour, or b) Laforgue did not, and/or c) the English-language poet who influenced Laforgue most was Walt Whitman, not particularly noted for his humour.

I would concede only the last point, reluctantly, for while Whitman may not be noted for his sense of humour, he certainly had one. In any event Laforgue did have a sense of humour, and the French generally do not. What the French have in abundance is wit, which is quite a different commodity. The French also love puns, and have a bawdy jocularity, ranging from François Rabelais (c. 1494–1553) to the comic actor Jacques Tati

(1907–1982) that can be highly amusing — but I can see this taking us too far afield.

Back to Laforgue. The poet chafed under academic discipline, failed all his university exams, and took great, almost wicked pleasure in experimenting with modern poetic forms, including Whitmanesque "free verse." He was, if you ask me, not nearly as "free" as the American poet — but better. Much appreciated in the 1880s, both in the literary salons of Paris and in the courts of Hohenlohe and Schlezwig-Holstein, where he tutored the Empress Augusta as well as some lesser princelings, the young, handsome, elegant, modern, and cosmopolitan poet became to nineteenth-century French letters what Jacques Offenbach (1819–1880) had been to nineteenth-century French music.

The ending was not happy. A year after their marriage, Laforgue and his English wife both died of consumption — tuberculosis — while still in their twenties. Unlike some Romantic poets who also died young — Keats, twenty-six, or Shelley, thirty, are obvious examples — Laforgue's modernist ouevre seems incomplete. His best poems, one feels, were still to come. Though far from forgotten, he may be remembered today for the English and American poets he influenced — T.S. Eliot, Ezra Pound — more than for his own work. Still, his magnum opus, *L'Imitation de Notre-Dame la Lune*, did appear in 2001 in a new translation by Peter Dale.

My version of Laforgue's much-anthologized "Winter, Approaching" is a free translation, though not nearly as free as some others in this collection. In spite of the liberties I have taken, I think the poet would easily recognize the poem as his own.

WINTER, APPROACHING

Forget about sitting down, the benches are too wet;
woods rust away but whirling leaves are still playing roulette,
the croupier of autumn favours red in every bet.
Foghorns intrude on shorelines and aggressively advance,
last Sunday we had not even a vestige of a chance
when reinforcement clouds came floating over from La Manche.

Fog pours in buckets.
The sea remits to the land its due
dropping liquid pennies into a leaf's deep pockets.
Hey, Sun-god! You, who in your chariot rode
past the troposphere to bomb with shafts of gold
your harvest: why did you implode?

At dusk, a moth-eaten Sun collapses on the hill
flops on his side, lacking the power or the will
to coalesce, and from a splash of yellow drool
rouse himself once again to be the one
that people call the Sun
instead of lying there and panting like a fool.
Hey, disc divine …
Kindly rise and shine!
Sun, over here, hello!
Oh I can't bear to listen any longer
to a cold furnace's faint echoes of thunder,

the grumblings of hunger
inside a hibernating fire-monger.

Away! Here old wolf winter waits
to mount his icy ambush in the wood
where his victims vanish without a trace,
look what happened to Little Red Riding Hood.
The trail of last month's oxcart, fossilized,
laboriously spreads across the plain,
above it gambol foolish flocks of clouds
en route to their transatlantic pen.
Rush, waste no time! It's a season we know
for gales that bury like rude lumberjacks
nests and small gardens deep beneath the snow
while fragile tree-bones crack under their ax.

Green sentinels, proud, at the forest's portal
just yesterday; now mortified and mortal,
gnarled, bent, weighed down, harassed, denuded
they leave unanswered the Grand Question: who did
ordain the red leaves' autumn dance,
the leaves, which disenchanted but no more deluded,
fall to nature as good lads fall for France?

Such a season, such a … Rust covers the cosmos.
On main routes where no one passes

brittle, half-eroded, pensive
telegraph wires in masses
sway in kilometer-envy.
The lumberjack-winds, being safe in the short run, relaxing,
sound their melancholy claxons:
winter prevails,
and jealous telegraph wires
        and scornful foghorn choirs
             merge with the northern gales.

This sound won't leave me ... what echoes, what a season!
Good-by harvest, say hello to the rain,
patiently knocking and staying and staining
      the windowpane again:
Hello rain, crimson leaves, wet benches, the reason
for saying farewell to baskets brimming with chestnuts.
Welcome phlegm, whooping cough, pulmonary disease,
as misery's mists settle on urban centres
      and historic rivers freeze.

(Oh, and what's more — pianos aside,
and forgetting about unseemly society capers —
are you aware of this recurring epidemic
of health statistics in the evening papers?)

Musset, de

ALFRED DE MUSSET'S SHORT life (1810–1857) began and ended in Paris. He crammed into it medical studies, political intrigue, a checkered career in the civil service, a celebrated affair with the Baroness Dudevant (a.k.a. George Sand) and an acquisition of "immortality" as a member of the French Academy. The last distinction was coupled with actual immortality, or at least longevity, as a Romantic playwright and poet. De Musset's plays continued to be revived in Europe well into the twentieth century, and Jean Renoir's great film, *The Rules of the Game* (*La règle du jeu, 1939*), was an updated version of his 1833 comedy of manners, *Les Caprices de Marianne*.

Everything being grist to a writer's mill, de Musset and George Sand each got a book out of their stormy affair; hers was called *Elle et lui*; his, *La Confession d'un Enfant du Siècle*. Both are worth reading still, though I doubt if many people do, as the prurient preference has long shifted to the Baroness Dudevant's affairs with men in the world of music: Franz Liszt and, especially, Frédéric Chopin. The Baroness, described as fat, common, and talkative by Baudelaire, managed to turn her handicaps into assets as she fornicated her way through the musical and literary establishment of civilized Europe, ending up as a friend of the great novelist Gustave Flaubert.

I do not know whether de Musset had the man-eating baroness in mind when he wrote his poem "*Sur une morte*," but her face (as seen in the famous painting by Eugène Delacroix) did flit through my mind when I started writing my variation on de Musset's theme for this collection. Far from being a translation, "The Lady as a Ship" bears no resemblance whatever to "Sur une morte" that inspired it, except for a thematic kinship.

THE LADY AS A SHIP

The lady wears such scars of time
As make her seem serene.
Sails furled, rails pearl'd, her prow sublime
    Regal she floats
Above the foam and brine.

Her face reveals none of the rage
The years have failed to soothe
Nor shows under the scabs of age
    As in repose
Her open wound of youth.

A few more lustrous hours to preen
Until her timbers crest.
A grim master appears below
    At whose behest
She'll mount the tidal flow.

Departure then, lifeboats adrift.
No promise, premise, proof, dolour.
The captain signals no distress:
    Takes off her soul,
Without unbuttoning her dress.

To illustrate how little my poem resembles the one that inspired it, here are de Musset's last lines from "*Sur une morte*":

Elle est morte, et n'a point vécu.
Elle faisait semblant de vivre.
De ses mains est tombé le livre
Dans lequel elle n'a rien lu.

Resemblance, anyone? Yes? No? Then how about resonance? Maybe?

Saint Ambrose

"THE PLAY'S THE THING," to borrow from Shakespeare. This being so, let us start with the thing itself — a.k.a. *das Ding an sich,* to borrow from Kant.

THE ROOSTER'S HYMN

Creator of the Universe,
Eternal father of the world,
Who time with time refurbishes,
Renewal without tedium:

Hear the vigilant guardian,
The chanticleer, whose hourly call
Divides the serpent of the night,
Sounding a new day's Te Deum.

The first to rise, the Morning Star,
Pierces through heaven's veil of gloom,

And lifts night's residue of murk,
Restoring equilibrium.

The cock's third crow renews the strength
Of sailors and turns back the tide,
The Church herself grows penitent:
Thomas doubted, Peter denied.

Rooster rouses the indolent,
Admonishes the somnolent,
Aurora's vocal complement
Will neither tire nor relent,

It raises hope, the rooster's song,
Exalts the weak, humbles the strong,
Exiles evils where they belong
And it reduces misery.

Jesus, if we are faltering,
Let malformed flowers of our ways
Wilt in your disapproving gaze,
And let tears wash away our sins.

Daybreak's effulgent hymn, redeem.
Jolt faint souls from a specious dream,
So we may enter, wide awake,
The Father's spacious atrium.

We are not certain when the bishop of Milan was born but he was around sixty, give or take a year, when he died on April 4 in 397. The fourth century clergyman, born in Gaul and educated in Rome, is considered one of the early church fathers and venerated accordingly, not only by Catholic but also by Lutheran and Greek Orthodox ecclesiastics. A man of enviable energy, his intrigue-filled, high-profile, and on the whole very successful corporate life as a church official, administrator, debater, and proselytizer, still left him enough time for scribbling, and he made important contributions to Christian theology as well as hymnody.

In my unfettered, though respectful, rendition of "*Aeterne rerum conditor,*" which is perhaps the best known of the great hymns written by the patron saint of busy bees, domestic animals and erudition, I retained his preferred poetic form: a simple but strict iambic tetrameter, unvarying, here sustained over eight stanzas. Some may find this rhythm tedious; I find it hypnotic.

In defence of calling my version unfettered but respectful, I offer this stanza as an example:

Gallo canente spes redit,
aegris salus refunditur,
mucro latronis conditur,
lapsis fides revertitur.

In my version:

It raises hope, the rooster's song,
Exalts the weak, humbles the strong,
Exiles evils where they belong
And it reduces misery.

Dedicated to the noble rooster, the hymn seems to indicate that the sainted author of *De bono mortis* (*On the Value of Death*) was an early riser. To accomplish everything he did, he pretty much had to be. Saint Augustine, one of Saint Ambrose's most prominent converts, considered it worth noting that the bishop of Milan did not move his lips while reading. Perhaps that's why he became the patron saint of erudition.

Rimbaud

MOVING SWIFTLY FROM SAINT to sinner, here's a sonnet from the greatest natural talent in Western poetry:

A MEAL IN CHARLEROI

After eight days of exercising the soles
of my footwear, hot, ravenous, tired,
I dropped by the Green Inn to inspect the holes
in my poor pair of boots before they expired,

then, sitting anyway, I ordered some slices
of bread and butter, with garlic ham, not too hot,
all I could afford at their exorbitant prices,
and when the girl brought the plate, I ate the lot.

I was happy, and she, with huge trays laden,
as pink and white as the ham, no less tasty,
poured me a beer with verve rather than style,

her eyes on the foam. Mine were on her waist. She
seemed a kissable stout Belgian maiden,
all billowing breasts and sunshine for a smile.

Arthur Rimbaud (1854–1891) was very pretty as a young boy,
and also exceptionally bright. A person so inclined might have
been torn between the impulse to read his poems and to have
sex with him — the poet Paul Verlaine did both. After a stormy,
absinthe-drenched, scandal-ridden, wild and brilliant career as
a poet, in the course of which he lived with, quarreled, recon-
ciled, traveled with, and had himself shot in the wrist by Verlaine,
the sullen youngster gave up writing at nineteen, enlisted in,
and promptly deserted from, the Dutch Colonial Army, then
knocked about in various Dutch and French possessions as a
clerk and a merchant, until he developed a carcinoma in his
knee, had his leg amputated, and returned to Fance to die at
the age of thirty-seven.

Considering that he did all his work in about four years,
between the ages of fifteen and nineteen, Rimbaud's impact on
world literature is little short of miraculous. The reason was his
prodigious talent, combined with the advantage of having taken
a seat at the right table for the literary roulette wheel. Paris in
the 1870s was high season for Western culture, and Rimbaud, a
rather bad boy, was a very good poet. I represent him here with
one free translation — "A Meal in Charleroi," above — and a
near parody: "A Sonnet of Vowels." Whatever they preserve of his
letter, I hope they both capture some of his spirit as a young rake.

A SONNET OF VOWELS

Black "A," red "E," green "U," blue "O." Vowels.
Someday, with passions spent and notes completed,
I may reveal your nativity's secret:
the shrieks, the pails of hot water, the towels

it took to clean after-birth's crimson mess.
Now antiseptic I's with icy lances
pierce fiercely through essential nuances
creating purple rage under duress

in pessimistic U's. The placid oceans
converge with forward-looking rural ventures
to warrant daring issues of debentures

of grazing fish and swimming cows. Promotions
proliferate. White lab-coats murmur Alpha.
Omega is her eyes. We plant alfalfa.

Catullus

READING RIMBAUD, MAKES ONE — at least, makes me — think of Catullus. Specifically, it makes me think of the following distich — or elegiac couplet, to be technical.

HATE AND LOVE

Odi et amo. Why? I have no answer. I've only the feelings.
That's how it is. My own heart crucifies me alive.

Gaius Valerius Catullus was born around 84 BC and died some thirty years later. He is probably the most widely read of all Roman poets today, though not the most skilled, influential, or significant. He may not even be the most erotic. He is, though, the most readable — and some would argue that in a writer that is all that counts.

I disagree. Readability is not all — but it is a lot.

The notorious "Lesbia" of Catullus's poems is believed to be the older and experienced sister of a conspiratorial politician named Publius Clodius Pulcher, who soon jilted the young poet, which inspired him to write "*Odi et Amo,*" among others. So many people have translated these two lines into so many languages that I would have felt horribly left out if I had not added my own version. If nothing else, it scans like the original.

CARMEN LXXXV

Odi et amo. Quare id faciam, fortasse requiris.
nescio, sed fieri sentio et excrucior.

What Catullus saw as Lesbia's treachery inspired longer poems as well, of course. My favorite is Carmen VIII.

DON'T MOPE, CATULLUS ...

Don't mope, Catullus, cope. My friend,
what's lost is lost. The day is gone.
The sun was up, now it is down,
the sky was bright, now it is dark,
life is like that. That's how it goes.
You led Lesbia by the hand,
Lesbia led you by the nose.
So be it. Never overstay a welcome,
don't ask for things you won't receive,
be like a stone rolling away
from her veranda. Take your leave.
If there are questions, let her ask them,
let her miss what's still there to miss,
be gone before she stumbles into
the hole she dug. It's her abyss.
Know when to fish. Know when to cut bait.
As life began, so life will end.
Lots of lips left to bite. It's not late.
Don't mope, Catullus. Cope, my friend.

The English version is my variation on the poet's theme. It is
no translation by any stretch of the imagination. I think Catullus
would recognize it, though. Here is the Latin:

CARMEN VIII

Miser Catulle, desinas ineptire,
et quod vides perisse perditum ducas.
fulsere quondam candidi tibi soles,
cum ventitabas quo puella ducebat
amata nobis quantum amabitur nulla.
ibi illa multa cum iocosa fiebant,
quae tu volebas nec puella nolebat,
fulsere vere candidi tibi soles.
nunc iam illa non vult: tu quoque impotens noli,
nec quae fugit sectare, nec miser viue,
sed obstinata mente perfer, obdura.
vale puella, iam Catullus obdurat,
nec te requiret nec rogabit invitam.
at tu dolebis, cum rogaberis nulla.
scelesta, vae te, quae tibi manet vita?
quis nunc te adibit? cui videberis bella?
quem nunc amabis? cuius esse diceris?
quem basiabis? cui labella mordebis?
at tu, Catulle, destinatus obdura.

I came to Catullus at a tender age because my parents were totally laissez-faire about my reading habits. Father believed in taking a horse to water, but not in trying to make it drink — and he believed even less in preventing a horse from drinking. No book in the house was compulsory or out of bounds.

Once a prissy visitor came into my room while I was doing my homework. She displayed no interest in my math exercises, but swooped down on an anthology entitled *Erotic Treasures*, containing poems by Catullus, bawdy bits by Chaucer, and excerpts from Boccaccio's *Decameron.*

"Well! Isn't the boy too young for that?" the visitor demanded, holding up the offending volume that detailed, among other risqué stories, the extramarital adventures of Florentine ladies during the plague years.

I was about twelve.

Father took the book out of her hand and put it back on my desk.

"When children are too young to read about sex, my dear," he said in his best baritone, "they don't. It bores them. When they're interested, they're not too young."

My father had no time for Mrs. Grundy and her ilk, but while he could win battles against her, he could not win the war. Prudery has great staying power. Mrs. Grundy went briefly out of fashion in the 1960s, only to return as Ms. Grundy in the 1970s. By then Father was entering his nineties, though, and had more pressing concerns.

Vergil

SINCE WE ARE IN Rome anyway, let us knock at a literary address next door. Vergil, spelled more often, but less accurately, as "Virgil," Publius Vergilius Maro (70 BC — 15 BC) is one of the great poets of antiquity. What he shares with other seminal figures of Western civilization is that no one reads him anymore — not counting, of course, the handful of scholars and academics who make a living out of reviewing, interpreting, annotating, and translating the classics.

In this collection, I took as my departure point a line in the conversation between Meliboeus and Tityrus in Vergil's *First Eclogue*, then promptly went from the idyllic pastoral world of the Roman poet to wherever my fancy took me. Galatea of the Marina is a creature of my imagination, not Vergil's, to say nothing about the buses in the square. Yet without Tityrus abandoning any hope of freedom and savings under Galatea's rule, a trigger Vergil pulled in the fifth stanza, my fancy would not have fired. "*Dum me Galatea tenebat, nec spes libertatis erat nec cura peculi*" is what my poem is about. "While Galatea held the reins, I hadn't much chance of hanging on to coins of currency or freedom."

GALATEA OF THE MARINA

… dum me Galatea tenebat,
nec spes libertatis erat nec cura peculi.

(Vergil)

1.

The day after she squandered his last dollar,
she smiled and brewed a splendid pot of tea,
he pondered by the jetty until sunrise.
Tityrus was he, and she, Galatea.

When buses started running in the square
he concluded throttling her was unwise
and writing her a letter not much better,
her extravagance wasn't even rare.

He asked the gods that no evil befall her,
and hoped that she might settle down in time;
his duty was to cope with her caprices,
gloss over things and cover her traces:
he did after all have another dime.

2.

Tityrus was he, and she, Galatea.
The day after she squandered his last quarter,
she smiled and brewed a splendid pot of tea,
he pondered by the jetty until sunrise.

When buses started running in the square
he concluded throttling her was unwise
and writing her a letter not much better,
a chevalier should be cavalier.

He thanked the gods that she was one of many,
and he should dance with her, for he had brought her,
it wasn't too late to pick up the pieces,
gloss over things and cover her traces:
he did after all have another penny.

3.

He pondered by the jetty until sunrise
the day after she squandered his last nickel;
Tityrus was he, and she, Galatea,
she smiled and brewed a splendid pot of tea.

When buses started running in the square
he concluded throttling her was unwise
and writing her a letter not much better,
let her spend his last gift unaware.

He thanked the gods at least she wasn't fickle,
he married her for worse the day he met her,
but even so, what once had been a trickle
was now a flood, and not a joking matter,
and so he said: "Old girl, put on a sweater,"

and by sunset buried her at sea.

Simonov

FAST-FORWARD ABOUT 2000 YEARS for a look at *odi et amo* in the modern era. Konstantin (born Kiril Mikhailovich) Simonov (1915–1979) was a strange mixture of seemingly incompatible elements: something of a matinee idol, a Soviet apparatchik, and the epitome of the patriotic soldier-poet. In the mould of the British Siegfied Sassoon and Rupert Brooke, or the Canadian Lt. Col. John McCrae, Simonov, too, was a front-line officer. He was a communist, naturally (no public figure could have been anything else in the Stalin-era) and as close to being a pulp magazine star in his steamy, semi-public love affair with the rising stage and screen star, Valentina Serova, as it was possible to be in Soviet society.

Valentina inspired Simonov's poem *"Zhdi Menya"* ("Wait For Me"). It had an impact on Russian-speaking readers during World War II not unlike the impact McCrae's "In Flanders Fields" had on English-speaking readers a generation earlier, during World War I — if not greater. The poem's lines were copied, cut out from newspapers, sent home in letters, inscribed on monuments, discovered in the pockets of the war-dead. To this day "Жди меня, и я вернусь ..." (Wait for me and I'll be back ...) is the Russian equivalent of "In Flanders fields the poppies blow ..."

Whether Simonov's muse, the actress Valentina, would have done what the poet exhorted loved ones to do — waited — was a different question. The answer is in some doubt; waiting is rarely the strong suit of movie stars. Be that as it may, I resisted the temptation to translate the poet's plea to his lover. I saw no reason to add another English version to the famous morale-boosting verse of The Great Patriotic War, Russian for the Second World War — "Zhdi Menya" exists in good English translations, including one by Mike Munford, available on the Web, which I was not sure I could improve or match. Simonov's poem, however, prompted me to write a variation on its theme: not as a parody, but in homage as well as in reply to the swashbuckling bard, the brave poet-soldier-lover, who was one of the very few non-monstrous figures to emerge from the Soviet period. I made the poem's narrator a pilot, in memory of Valentina's late husband, Spanish civil war flying ace, Anatoly Serov.

WAIT FOR ME: A SOVIET PILOT SPEAKS

Today we had warmer weather.
After some brackish rain pelted
down the trenches, the ice melted,
I received your Dear John letter.

Surprised, you ask? Well, yes, very,
given that I had no inkling
there was anything the matter.
I suppose I was deluded.

No harsh word, never a quarrel,
and now I feel like a blinking
idiot, inside a barrel
overturned, exposed, denuded.

"Wait for me," poets are prating.
They're in Moscow celebrating
"zhdi menya." Like hell you're waiting,
you have better things to do.

Well, c'est la guerre, as the French say,
or is it c'est la bloody vie.
There is only one slight problem.
While you, bitch, are making merry

with my best friend or some clever
service-dodger or whoever,
my hurt is too much to carry,
not a fucking thing to soothe it,

no antidote, no medicine
no balm, no apothecary.
Oh, never mind. Time to move out.
Gear up. Have a go at Jerry.

Juhász

WHILE ON THE SUBJECT of feeling suicidal, Gyula Juhász was born in 1883 and it took him until 1937 to kill himself. It was not for want of trying. A 1907 attempt to throw himself into the Danube from Budapest's picturesque Chain Bridge was interrupted by a passing girlfriend, Ilona Klima, who told the young man that his first book of poems had just been published in his native city of Szeged. This kept him going until 1914, when he shot himself in the chest at the National Hotel in Budapest. He survived to see the publication of his next book in 1915, and was officially declared insane only in 1917 after being hospitalized following another incident. In 1919 he supported the short-lived Communist dictatorship, after the collapse of which he lost his job as a provincial high school teacher and eked out a meager living as a freelance journalist for the rest of his life, which lasted until 1937 when he ended it with an overdose of sleeping pills at the age of fifty-four.

The great love of the poet's life, a small-town actress named Anna Sárvári, rejected him rather unceremoniously, thereby ensuring her own immortality. Her grand refusal inspired the Anna-cycle, some of the most moving and memorable love poems in Hungarian, or perhaps in any language. People enjoyed the poems but no one blamed the actress for refusing the poet; by the time they met in 1908, he was as crazy as a hoot owl. The 1914 love poem "I Don't Remember..." from the Anna-cycle is probably as faithful a translation as I have ever done (which isn't saying much).

I DON'T REMEMBER ...

I don't remember how blonde was her blondness,
all I know is that fields of wheat are fair,
and in summertime's sizzling sunlight I sense
in fields of wheat, the tincture of her hair.

I don't recall the blue of her eyes' blueness,
until departing September's surprise:
deep in the whirling autumn sky's lacunas
glows the cerulean blue of her eyes.

I waited for her words to fall like manna.
I don't recall them, but when meadows sigh
in spring, I hear the gentle words of Anna
from a far-off spring, as distant as the sky.

If money, love, and happiness eluded Juhász, success and appreciation did not. The public, and perhaps especially his peers, thought highly of his work. Viewed as a "poet's poet," he won the prestigious Baumgarten Prize three years running, in 1929, 1930, and 1931. This success caused him to suffer a nervous breakdown and enter a sanatorium.

The poem "The Sermon" in this collection is inspired by Juhász's magnificent "Sermon on the Mount," but other than the theme and perhaps the mood it bears no resemblance to it. I asked myself what would have happened if Goethe had read Juhász in the original Hungarian and, liking it, had written his own variation on the theme, in his own voice, in German. So the poem in this book is my English translation of the imaginary German poem that Juhász's actual Hungarian poem might have inspired (but of course did not) in Goethe. The automotive equivalent would be an artist's drawing of a Citroën-Maserati, I suppose.

THE SERMON

The moonlit lake
The boats afloat
Men ship the oars
Lower the sails
The women sit
Without a sound.
The people wait.

On pebbled shores
A fire burns
Pale drifts the smoke.
The master's late.

Evils abound.

Where are you Lord?
Lord are you ill
Or *are* you, still?

Low shrubs surround
The hillside bare
The stride is long
The summit far

The master's robe
Touches the ground.

Sea-anchors set.
Embers in urns.
Fish in the net.
All heads are bent
All eyes are closed
The master turns.

The face is gaunt
The beard unkempt
The robe is rent
The gait is odd
The gestures daunt.

Jesus the God.

The Son of Man
His Father sent
To plant a seed
Doesn't relent
Doesn't depart
And words follow
To stop the heart
Confound the wise

Dash down the hard
Exalt the meek.

The last breeze dies.
The holy flame
Glows on the Mount.

Evils recede.

Trakl

LET'S STAY WITH INSANITY for another round. Georg Trakl
(1887–1914) was born a Protestant in Catholic Salzburg, but this
probably would not have driven him mad. His mother's genes
are the better suspects. Maria, the wife of hardware merchant
Tobias Trakl, was what in our days some people might call
"creative." Nineteenth-century Austrians would have described
her, more accurately, as "theatrical." In addition to an eye for
drawing and an ear for music, Maria also had a knack for
depression and withdrawal.

Her children were not far behind. By the early 1900s her
son had turned from a moody, difficult teenager into a restless,
drug-dependent adult. Possibly an undiagnosed schizophrenic
and definitely an alcohol-, opium-, and chloroform-addict, young
Georg may have had an incestuous relationship with his simi-
larly drug-dependent sister, Grete. Half a century before hippies
came along, Trakl behaved like one: he dropped out, tuned in,
and turned on. He wore eccentric clothes, smoked opium, put
on bohemian airs. After leaving, or rather abandoning, school
in 1905, he flirted with every fad of modernity on stage and in

literature. He wrote plays and poetry, neither too well nor too successfully, while working as an apprentice pharmacist, perhaps to gain easier access to drugs.

His father's death in 1911 left the family destitute. Poverty, obviously, did not improve matters. The only thing that distinguished Trakl from other tiresome, touchy, emotionally and financially needy bohemians was genuine talent — but it did not distinguish him enough. Although a group of avant garde writers around the influential literary journal *Der Brenner* — including editor Ludwig von Ficker and the writer Franz Werfel — recognized and promoted him, Trakl continued wrestling with his demons. The Edwardian hippie's progress was marked by published books, pharmaceutical studies, military service, and suicide attempts. In 1914, hospitalized in Poland where he had been posted with his Austrian army unit, Trakl made his exit. He did so just a few days before the philosopher Ludwig Wittgenstein, who had settled a sizeable amount of money on him, had been due to arrive for a visit. "The tone of true genius," as Wittgenstein once described him, died (accidentally or intentionally) of an overdose of cocaine, self-administered. He was twenty-seven. His sister, Grete, shot herself three years later.

The gentle Austrian madman's influence on German letters ebbs and flows, but on the whole it lingers. Nearly one hundred years after his death, his name elicits 142,000 responses on the Internet. The expressionist poet still has the capacity to impress. (Pun, such as it is, intended.) Few would dispute that some of his lines are magnificent.

"Evening Song" is a straightforward translation of a Trakl poem, one of perhaps half-a-dozen straightforward translations in this book.

EVENING SONG

At evening we trudge along darkening trails,
Tracking our own pale specters.

When thirsty,
We taste in the white water of the lake
Our sad childhood's sweetness.

When dead, we rest under the elder bushes,
Watching grey seagulls.

Springtime clouds float above the shadowy town
Whose cloistered silence recalls a nobler age.

When I took your narrow hand in mine
Your round eyes opened wide.
That was long ago.

Still, when dark notes haunt the soul,
You loom white in a friend's autumn landscape.

"Second Evening Song" is my variation on what I take to be Trakl's theme in the same poem — making it (for better or worse) the poem Trakl might have written, instead of the one he did write, if he had been me. Stealing Trakl's egg and incubating it in my nest would be another way of putting it.

SECOND EVENING SONG

Recollecting in the fading waste
of dissolution, dissonance, decay
childhood enchantments of a sweeter taste,
old invitations, innocent, to play,
as when I covered your small hand with mine,
is only treading water over time.

So, too, observing old towns in decline
under flapping cloud canopies of spring,
or watching greedy seagulls wheel and climb
above foam-speckled pebbles, sunset-red,
the boulder-fringed graves of the seaside dead,
is only treading water over time.

When darker notes begin to haunt his soul
Man conjures cryptic images in white
refurbishing the landscape of his fall,

as trudging along darkening paths home,

he trails a pallid specter. It's his own.

Swan songs only tread water over time.

The final poem, "In Memoriam," is my homage to Trakl, using some of his imagery.

IN MEMORIAM

The poet of the unpredictable,

thin autumn sun; blue spaces; elder trees

inhabited by silence; extinct angels;

God's golden eyes over a place of skulls;

the poet of no rhymes and fewer reasons,

the poet-pharmacist, the insane Austrian,

who in the lonely hours of the soul

found it pleasant to saunter in the sun;

the poet, who never successfully fended

for himself, or mended history, but tended

the war-wounded in Poland, and befriended

Franz Werfel and Ludwig Wittgenstein;

the poet of dependence, drug-driven,

born as 1887 began,

dead in 1914 at twenty-seven,

and likely without a fixed address in heaven:

as long as he's still served by memory's morgue,

let us look in on poor Trakl, Georg.

Heltai

FOR TOTAL CONTRAST, THE sanest poet in this volume is probably Jenõ Heltai (1871–1957). The nephew of Israel's founding father was one of those writers whose works are better known than their names. In Hungary thousands could recite Heltai's lyrics of the musical *János Vitéz* without recognizing the name of the man who wrote them, just as in Britain or in America many would know of the book (or film) *Goodbye Mr. Chips* who have never heard the name of its author, James Hilton (1900–1954). Some writers loom larger than their works; some remain smaller. Virginia Woolf would be an example of the first; Heltai is an example of the second.

After abandoning his legal studies, Heltai, like his uncle, the Zionist visionary Theodor Herzl, worked as a journalist. When he tired of being an ink-stained wretch, however, instead of switching to politics, he became a playwright, lyricist, theatre director, and itinerant press correspondent, filing stories from Paris, London, Vienna, Berlin, and Istanbul. He wrote, as he lived, with a light touch; he was popular, even celebrated, but underestimated. It seems that in literature, just as in life, one has to take oneself seriously before anyone else will. Characteristically, the French, who appreciate a light touch more than other Europeans, awarded Heltai the *Légion d'honneur* for his sparkling translations well before his own country gave him a major literary prize — in the nick of time, too, just before he passed away at the age of eighty-six.

"On Observing a Gaggle of Geese" is my homage to Heltai, written in his manner.

ON OBSERVING A GAGGLE OF GEESE

The old gander chases a goose,
oh, will she run or will she stop?
Is passion blind? Is it obtuse?
Will Madam yield? Will she refuse?

Is this a start? Is this the lot?
Will their love hurt? Will it amuse?
A deal, perhaps? Goose gets a cut?
Let us be calm and read the clues.

It's too unnerving. What's the use?
Can't go to bed, not knowing what
is blacker, the kettle or the pot.
Is Cupid tightening the noose

or about to eat an apricot?
I hear a dreadful noise. My God,
a heart just broke. I wonder whose?
Is it the gander gone? The goose?

Baudelaire

TO MOVE FROM THE bearable to the unbearable lightness of being — with apologies to Milan Kundera — Charles Pierre Baudelaire was given forty-six years on Earth to put his mark indelibly on world literature, which he did. Few poets or critics had more influence in their time and, especially, soon after their time, than this substance-addicted son of a French civil servant and art-loving dilettante. Born in 1821, and dead by 1867, Baudelaire's working life was even shorter, because after finishing his studies it took him six years to publish his first art criticism, another twelve to publish his first book, and then he was sidelined by a massive stroke for two years before his death. However, in the quarter century left to him between his graduation (1839) and debilitation (1865) he pretty much set the tone of the movements in art as well as literature that were to be dominant until nearly our own day: modernism and symbolism, along with their various siblings and descendants.

The remark "we all emerged from Gogol's cloak" has been attributed to Dostoyevsky. He was referring to the influence Nikolai Gogol's satirical ghost story, "The Cloak," published in

1842, had on Russian writers of his generation. One might with similar justification say that French, or indeed Western, literature in the late nineteenth to mid-twentieth century emerged from Baudelaire's 1857 book of poetry, *Les fleurs du mal* or *The Flowers of Evil*. And even those who find this far-fetched would probably concede that Euro-American literature's centerpieces for the next hundred years included many flowers (and some weeds) that had been gathered by the syphilitic and opium-smoking art critic.

Several writers and scholars explored Baudelaire's aesthetic influence on English-language literature, most notably T.S. Eliot and Edmund Wilson. I am not proposing to add to their insights and observations, or to repeat the oft-told tale of Baudelaire's life and loves. My two Baudelaire-variations in this book are free translations, with "The Flip Side" being freer than "The Balcony," which is free enough.

THE FLIP SIDE

Angel of sunny days, do you know of the blues?
The fear, the boredom, the shame, the obtuse
self-flagellation? And do you wonder whose
doing it is that you're so terse with a stranger?
Do you know your flip side, high-spirited angel?

Angel of goodwill, what do you know of hate?
A vengeful virtue which, were it your estate,

would send you with clenched fist and stiffened gait
to slaughter baby Jesus in the manger.
Do you know your flip side, charitable angel?

Angel of health, do you know of disease,
whose fevers wrestle giants to their knees?
Green hospice walls muffle despairing pleas.
See a woman cringe as pain comes to derange her:
meet illness. It's your flip side, wholesome angel.

Glamorous angel of mischievous twinkles
in eyes of promised pleasures — what do you know of wrinkles?
But wrinkles know you. Past face cream and blinkers,
revulsion is the next stop. Your old age will
become the flip side of your beauty, angel.

And you, luminous spirit of eternal bliss,
confer enchantment before the abyss:
King David on his deathbed asked for this.
But fortunes reverse, magic flees, fates betray.
For me, angel of bliss, do nothing. Only pray.

Some regard "*Le Balcon*," from the *Black Venus* cycle, as the
most beautiful love poem in French. I include it here. Should any-
one wish to make the same claim for it in English, I won't object.

LE BALCON

Mère des souvenirs, maîtresse des maîtresses,
Ô toi, tous mes plaisirs! ô toi, tous mes devoirs!
Tu te rappelleras la beauté des caresses,
La douceur du foyer et le charme des soirs,
Mère des souvenirs, maîtresse des maîtresses!

Les soirs illuminés par l'ardeur du charbon,
Et les soirs au balcon, voilés de vapeurs roses.
Que ton sein m'était doux! que ton coeur m'était bon!
Nous avons dit souvent d'impérissables choses
Les soirs illuminés par l'ardeur du charbon.

Que les soleils sont beaux dans les chaudes soirées!
Que l'espace est profond! que le coeur est puissant!
En me penchant vers toi, reine des adorées,
Je croyais respirer le parfum de ton sang.
Que les soleils sont beaux dans les chaudes soirées!

La nuit s'épaississait ainsi qu'une cloison,
Et mes yeux dans le noir devinaient tes prunelles,
Et je buvais ton souffle, ô douceur! ô poison!
Et tes pieds s'endormaient dans mes mains fraternelles.
La nuit s'épaississait ainsi qu'une cloison.

Je sais l'art d'évoquer les minutes heureuses,
Et revis mon passé blotti dans tes genoux.
Car à quoi bon chercher tes beautés langoureuses
Ailleurs qu'en ton cher corps et qu'en ton coeur si doux?
Je sais l'art d'évoquer les minutes heureuses!

Ces serments, ces parfums, ces baisers infinis,
Renaîtront-ils d'un gouffre interdit à nos sondes,
Comme montent au ciel les soleils rajeunis
Après s'être lavés au fond des mers profondes?
— Ô serments! ô parfums! ô baisers infinis!

THE BALCONY

Mother of memories, mistress of mistresses,
my desire's due and your devotion's duty;
you, the source of sweet yeses and caresses,
the charm of days and the evenings' beauty,
mother of memories, mistress of mistresses.

Those evenings with the heat of coals aglow,
the balcony suffused in rosy vapours,
imperishable words appear to flow,
and hands embark on exploratory capers.
Those evenings with the heat of coals aglow.

Is there beauty like twilight, copper-plated,
the bronze of space spiced with your blood's perfume?
The king of dusk looks at his queen, elated,
waiting for his heart's beating to resume.
Is there beauty like twilight, copper-plated?

We let the night surround us like a shelter
but eyes still sense where the other's glance lingers;
the sweet poison of breaths mingling to melt where
(your toes asleep in my brotherly fingers)
we let the night surround us like a shelter.

Evoking memories? I know the art.
My past is curled up in your lap. It dwells there.
You live in your firm body, tender heart,
why would I seek your languorous beauty elsewhere?
Evoking memories: I know the art.

Will hints of scents, promises, endless kisses
ever return? Can our passion's banshees
rise shrieking, after ardour's skirmishes,
as laundered suns emerge daily from profound seas?
Oh, hints of scents. Promises. Endless kisses.

Ady

THE DANUBIAN BAUDELAIRE, HUNGARY'S syphilitic genius, had even fewer years in which to make his mark, but he did. In cultures where poetry counts, such as Hungary's, the public often identifies an entire epoch with a poet. Such iconic figures are halfway between literary deities and matinee idols — which may not prevent their adoring public from cheerfully letting them starve. One might call it worshipful neglect.

Emperor Franz Joseph's generation cast Endre Ady (1877–1919) in this role. It was, of course, a temporary position; after the First World War, Regent Miklós Horthy's generation replaced him with Attila József (1905–1937.) The language of both has been described as "the mother tongue" of Hungarian poetry: Ady's during the first quarter of the twentieth century, and József's during the second quarter. Neither poet starved, though József came close. (An earlier bard to make a similar impact on an entire generation was Sándor Petőfi, the voice of the 1848 revolution against Habsburg Austria. He was a Hungarian super-patriot, ironically of Slovakian descent.)

Ady was also a super-patriot, but of the conflicted kind, alternately cursing and blessing his compatriots. Born in the village of Érdmindszent (now called Ady Endre, Romania) in what was then Austro-Hungarian Transylvania, Ady came from a family of impoverished gentry, complete with a family crest and "dog-skin" (patent of nobility) but no land or bank account. A Catholic born of a Calvinist mother, Ady attended first a Calvinist and later a Catholic gymnasium. He was an indifferent and unruly student. At university he read jurisprudence, then abandoned the study of law, published his first book of poems, and from the age of twenty-two lived as a journalist-cum-bohemian — alcoholic, libertine, and eventually syphilitic — in the cities of Nagyvárad, Transylvania (now Oradea); Budapest, Hungary; and Paris, France. He died of syphilis at forty-two.

Ady's poetry initiated a literary revolution in pre-First World War Hungary, especially following its first appearance (1908) in the influential periodical *Nyugat* (*The West*). By the time of the First World War, Ady was the nation's unofficial poet laureate. His "public" poems were as subjective and lyrical as his "private" ones; his great loves, Adél and Berta, found their way into his poetry as "Léda" and "Csinkszka." Like a sponge (or perhaps just like a journalist) Ady absorbed the political and literary trends that were current in his time and place, then regurgitated them in a tone uniquely his own. His poetry, an Oriental bazaar in an Occidental outpost set up at the junction of the nineteenth and twentieth centuries, was a jumble of socialist, nationalist, romantic, ethnocentric, and irredentist notions, coexisting almost harmoniously with the contrary ideas of modernists, impressionists, Parnassists, pacifists, classicists, psychoanalysts, and the exponents of *l'art pour l'art*. Ady had a way of presenting every item in his hypnotically individual voice, as if he had just thought of it himself. What he said was often second-hand, but how he said it was usually tailor-made. Considering that he was a poet rather than a philosopher, he gave value for money.

My version of his famous poem "*Álmodik a nyomor*" ("Misery Dreams") is a translation: free, but not straying too far from the original. It is the only Ady poem I have ever translated. Much as I could see the *fin-de-siècle* icon's mesmeric power, his poetry always struck me as much Ady about nothing.

MISERY DREAMS

Lush ballrooms, lounges, supper clubs,
tuxedos, crinolines,
hush, look. In some nearby slum
upon a mattress on the floor
misery dreams.

A bleak, factory-ravaged lad,
hollow-chested, he glints
as smudges of cold moisture sit
on his lips. As royal as
a sleeping prince

he dreams for himself a girl, a bowl
of fruit, both washed; a deep
dish of soup, fresh linen.
He dreams of running water, then
laughs in his sleep.

He dreams of coughing up less blood
and of the day he can afford
some meat, and dreams another year
will pass until he must appear
before the Lord.

City, pause for a few minutes,
taste not your caviar and cream,
and leave your champagne flutes unfilled.
In some nearby slum, misery
dreams its last dream.

József

HAVING BROUGHT UP HIS name, we might as well continue with his entry. Whether or not Attila József was the greatest Hungarian poet of all times, as some insist, there is little doubt that he was a great poet. This, in spite (or perhaps because) of being mentally ill. He did recover from a bout of Marxism, but as he also suffered from what may have been bipolar disorder or schizophrenia, this was not sufficient to cure him. Born into a working-class family in 1905 — mother, a laundress, father, a soap-maker who vanished after emigrating to Teddy Roosevelt's America — he grew up and lived in poverty until his death, of attempted self-mutilation, in 1937.

His short poems echoed here, "Mother," "Self-Portrait," and "Hopelessly," are all fairly straightforward, albeit free, translations. They follow the form and content of the originals as closely as my skills and the vagaries of inspiration permit.

MAMA

Week after week mama is on my mind.
I step, I stop. I hear shuffling behind.
Her laundry-basket creaks. The mangling stone.
She's off to the attic, leaving me on my own.

I start bawling (then still a man of candour)
I stomp my feet, throw tantrums, I demand her.
Pick me up, carry me! My hurt is dramatic.
Forget the bloated wash. Take me to the attic.

Mama never scolds, just fills up the hamper,
Linens billow on the tides of the damp air.
If she would only turn and look at me once!
She keeps folding the sheets without a glance.

My whine has become permanent. She's silent.
Her shadow fills the firmament. A giant.
Her gray hair floats as she bends to apply
More blueing mix. Mama rinses the sky.

SELF-PORTRAIT

A cheerful soul, he was benign,
if pig-headed when feeling wronged.
Enjoyed his food. Some even saw
in him a faint likeness of God.
A Jew doctor gave him a coat,
his relatives, sufficient rope
to hang himself. The Eastern Rites
supplied a priest. Comfort he did without.
The self-destruction that he wrought
was transnational in scope,

but don't give it another thought.

HOPELESSLY

(slowly, thoughtfully)

A man's journey ends when he reaches
a kind of sad, waterlogged plain
resembling vast and empty beaches.
He looks around, nods, can't sustain

much hope. I try looking around
likewise, casual and relaxed.
Birch leaves reveal, without a sound,
the silvery swish of the ax.

My heart sits far out on a limb
of nothingness, shivering. I let it.
There's nowhere for it to climb.
Tame stars gather to stare at it.

The reader might want to know that I couldn't resist commenting on the last poem while translating it: "My heart sits far out on a limb/ of nothingness, shivering. I let it," isn't quite accurate. József did not "let it." I did.

The poem "Consciousness" is my variation on a theme by the poet, though it borrows so much from József that it almost amounts to a free translation — almost, but not quite.

If the poem puzzles some readers they may take it as an indication that they are not Marxists or schizophrenics. József was both.

By the time he wrote "Consciousness," ideas and images were heaped upon one another like firewood in his own consciousness, each piece pressing upon and determining the next. The poem is a panorama of existence as seen by a man in a dungeon: a homeless man, literally as well as figuratively, writing at a time when advancing mental illness was making him see connections between unrelated things. He suffered from a hypertrophy of cause and effect. For instance, he considered yellow the colour of insanity. Once, while institutionalized, he complained to his older sister Jolán (he called her "Lucie" in correspondence) that he was being made to eat roast duck despite everybody knowing that a duck was a yellow bird. Blotches of yellow, however, when combined with red and blue, would appear balanced as order to him — a kind of Danubian Ying and Yang. He saw a cold and precise world that would overlook him as insufficiently lyrical for a poet and reject him as much too lyrical for a lover; not let him graduate from school for being much too communist and expel him from the Party for not being communist enough. For a child in foster care; for a street urchin stealing coal from freight trains; and earlier, for a preschooler teased for taking the family's pet chicken to the dump on a string, his single mother being too poor to buy chickenfeed, happiness appeared as a weighty affair, a shapeless blonde in the mud, all fluffed up and making piggish noises.

József's disease used to be called paranoid schizophrenia: a condition that makes a patient's mind resemble a conspiracy theorist's. In his world everything fits. Winners load shiny heaps of black coal into freight cars, while losers squat by the tracks, waiting for precious pieces to fall off. It is a nasty voyage but, as the French poet Mallarmé put it in a different context, "Listen to the sailors sing!" If the tune depresses, that's the poet's problem; the reader's delight is how he sings it (assuming my variation can convey it at all.)

CONSCIOUSNESS

Dawn separates earth from the sky,
a fissure, gentle, life-revealing,
at whose razor-sharp command
children and insects twirl into being.
There is no moisture in the air,
a sparkling lightness levitates;
during the night, like butterflies,
little leaves settled on the trees.

I dreamt of blue, red, and yellow
blotches. They amounted to order,
accounting for each speck of dust.
Sneaking across a murky border,
now order flows molten in my limbs.
The moon climbs. The day has begun
in a universe in reverse.
At night inside me shines the sun.

A thin man, I subsist on bread,
prayed for once and eaten twice,
hoping one day to throw for it
something more substantial than dice.
Rump roasts don't rub against my lips,
I am what my fortune allows.
Even the cleverest cat, indoors,
can't catch a harvest mouse.

Like a pile of split wood, the world
is heaped upon itself. At rest,
each piece squeezes, clutches, eludes,
infests and determines the next.
That which is not, will sport a bush,
that which will be, slyly increases,
that which is, is a thing of the past,
it wilts, changes colour, falls to pieces.

Inside the freight yard, flat against
a soot-sodden tree's roots, I crouched.
Strange-tasting, sharp-edged, semi-sweet
industrial weeds touched my mouth.
I kept my eyes on the guard's stubborn
shadow, as he, well-fed and tough,
kept jumping between shiny heaps
of coal. What was he thinking of?

Misery lives inside. Outside
only misery's explanation.
Wounded souls festering in fever
are easy to diagnose. Creation.
Cause and effect. Logic and order.
No one can come into his own
by cutting wood and mixing mortar
to build his miserly landlord a home.

From underneath the night, watching
revolving sky's cogwheel: a patient,
majestic loom of bygone times
weaving luminous legislation
from the delicate threads of chance
I marveled, till past misty dreams
I noticed the fabric of the law
keeps coming apart at the seams.

Silence listened closely. The clock
struck one. My anger spent,
why not re-visit youth, I thought,
the peeling walls of wet cement
where I knew freedom. And a flock
of constellations, planets, Mars,
watched me scramble to my feet.
The stars sparkled like prison bars.

Iron can weep and rain can laugh.
I heard them both. The past can split.
A man can forget, if only what
he conjures up. Life is not it.
Nature affords me no choice
I love till I run out of steam.
Why should I have to forge a sword
of you, my precious self-esteem?

A grown-up person, who at last
has learned to sit back, not to fret;
who knows: life is the appetizer
before the main course of death;
who clings to no host, parent, priest,
but drinks his soup, and then, replete,
rises politely, leaves the table,
and lets the waiter clear his plate.

I recall seeing happiness.
She was soft, blonde, and weighed a ton.
Across the implacable grass
swaying her way with great aplomb,
plunking her curly smile in a
lukewarm puddle, she called for rough
play. I still see the hesitant
moonlight fiddling with her fluff.

I live near the tracks. Trains
come and go here. When one passes
rows of bright windows disrupt
evening's fluttering semi-darkness.
That's how illuminated days
hurtle through endless night's reprise.
Lit up by each private compartment,
I lean on my elbow. Keep my peace.

Lope de Vega

A REFRESHING DIP INTO the swimming pool of time washes off the grime of the twentieth century. Unlike Shakespeare in style and personality — unlike, indeed, in most ways, except stature — Felix Lope de Vega y Carpio (1562–1635) is to Spaniards what the Bard is to Englishmen: an icon, symbolic of the spirit and culture of the nation. Spain has actually two such icons, Miguel de Cervantes (1547–1616) being the other. It is uncanny that they lived overlapping lives.

Lope de Vega's gifts, like Shakespeare's, have been amply distributed through concept and idiom even among those of his compatriots who have never read a line of his plays and poems. Equally prolific in his literary output and romantic liaisons, the Spanish bard earned a bestselling writer's living from his first occupation, and a most-wanted fugitive's exile from the second. Neither fortune nor misfortune stopped him from authoring an estimated fifteen hundred-plus full-length plays, from pastoral and historic romances to comedies. Over four hundred survive, and two or three, such as *Fuente Ovejuna* and *El Perro del Hortelano,* are frequently revived. According to legend, Lope de

Vega wrote his incendiary three-acter, *Fuente Ovejuna,* in a single night. On a bet, as a student, I tried to copy it out in one night, by candlelight, using a quill, as Lope de Vega must have: I didn't even come close.

A natural dramatist as well as a natural lyricist, Lope de Vega merges the two strains to achieve almost filmic effects in some of his sonnets. Such is "Judith's Triumph," whose fourteen lines recount Apocrypha's famous episode of a fierce Hebrew maiden seducing and beheading the Assyrian general laying siege to her city. In my free translation I resist the temptation to render Lope de Vega's sonnet as a film script. Others may not be so reticent.

JUDITH'S TRIUMPH

Inside the tent, a horrid shoulder
sags from the bed to the floor.
Outside, dying campfires smoulder
beneath Bethulia's wall.

Bethulia's besieger, the tyrant,
is a trunk enmeshed in a sheet
turning slowly to ice. Wine-stained, silent,
useless guards in a heap.

Inside the tent, half-empty vessels,
agony's aura, passion's scorch-
marks, blood-spots on silken tassels.

Outside, high on the wall, emerging
from a cheering throng, a Hebrew virgin
brandishes a head, like a torch.

Ronsard, de

ONCE WE ARE IN the sixteenth century, we might as well stay there
for a moment.

LAST POEM

Leaving it all behind: the house, the garden,
the gilded vessels and the burnished urns,
to sing, as dying swans do, when departing
the darkening lake where the river turns.

It's done. The plush yarn spins off the spindle,
I've lived, I've flown, I've sung, I'm on my way.
My quill scratches the sky. New flames kindle.
New knights will pass, with new dragons to slay.

It's good to stand aside; better to rest
in the primeval void; but it's best
to join Jesus the Christ's heavenly choir,

discarding earthly fabrics of decay

in which fate and fortune dress up to play

and soar as spirits, cleansed of mud and mire.

His contemporaries referred to Pierre de Ronsard (1524–1585) as the Prince of Poets. Later generations called him simply "Ronsard." His name became synonymous with poetry, although he was a professional courtier as well, first in the service of Madeleine of France, who married Scotland's James the Fifth, and later in the entourage of the Duke of Orleans. In fact, Ronsard came from a family of well-connected courtiers, and had it not been for physical infirmity, beginning with early-onset deafness, he might have been remembered as a successful diplomat. As it was, he had to settle for being one of the giants of world literature.

Ronsard's odes and elegies have dated somewhat along with their genres, but his sonnets are as readable today as they were over four hundred years ago, when the king's sister, Marguerite de Valois, snatched his book from the hands of a rival poet who tried to mock him, and read the poems herself to the applause of the court. Centuries later, it was a sonnet by Ronsard that inspired W. B. Yeats to write one of his finest poems in English. (His example influenced my approach to several of the poems in this book.)

First, Ronsard's original from *Sonnets pour Hélène* published in 1587:

QUAND VOUS SEREZ BIEN VIEILLE ...

Quand vous serez bien vieille, au soir, à la chandelle,
Assise auprès du feu, dévidant et filant,
Direz, chantant mes vers, en vous émerveillant:
Ronsard me célébrait du temps que j'étais belle.

Lors, vous n'aurez servante oyant telle nouvelle,
Déjà sous le labeur à demi sommeillant,
Qui au bruit de mon nom ne s'aille réveillant,
Bénissant votre nom de louange immortelle.

Je serai sous la terre et fantôme sans os:
Par les ombres myrteux je prendrai mon repos:
Vous serez au foyer une vieille accroupie,

Regrettant mon amour et votre fier dédain.
Vivez, si m'en croyez, n'attendez à demain:
Cueillez dès aujourd'hui les roses de la vie.

And here is Yeats' variation on Ronsard's theme:

WHEN YOU ARE OLD

When you are old and grey and full of sleep,
And, nodding by the fire, take down this book,
And slowly read, and dream of the soft look
Your eyes had once, and of their shadows deep.

How many loved your moments of glad grace
And loved your beauty with love false or true,
But one man loved the pilgrim soul in you,
And loved the sorrows of your changing face.

And bending down beside the glowing bars,
Murmur, a little sadly, how Love fled
And paced upon the mountain overhead
And hid his face amid a crowd of stars.

— W.B. Yeats in his 1893 collection *The Rose*.

I paraphrased Ronsard's "Last Poem" in this collection in the manner of Yeats — that is, I tried to write it in my own manner, as Yeats turned Ronsard's poem into his own.

Storm

"IT IS JUST A small ordinary town, my birthplace; it lies on a flat treeless coastal plain and its houses are old and grey ... Yet I've always thought of it as a pleasant place," wrote fifty-one-year-old Theodor Storm in 1868. Storm had no way of knowing that an elegy to his birthplace, Husum, a grey town by the grey North Sea, would become my constant companion about eighty years later. My father decided to put "*Die Stadt*" to music, and he sang it at least once a week during the 1950s, accompanying himself on the Bechstein piano.

Storm, regarded by many as Prussia's foremost poet, suited my father temperamentally. In addition to a taste for *Hochdeutsch* — high German — they shared a curious mixture of individualistic romanticism and disciplined, indeed resigned, wisdom. An attitude rather than a philosophy, it entailed a slightly mocking but genuine and principled acceptance of everyday virtues and realities. The bard of Schleswig-Holstein (1817–1888) and my father (1883–1972) were about two generations apart, but they were both bourgeois bohemians, a contradiction epitomized by Goethe but exhibited by lesser mortals as well. Stylistically, Storm was at home in his period far more than my father, whose work was often musically anachronistic — his *Lied* of Storm's most famous poem, while tuneful and attractive, was rather out of joint with its times. Here is Storm's original first:

DIE STADT

Am grauen Strand, am grauen Meer
Und seitab liegt die Stadt;
Der Nebel drückt die Dächer schwer,
Und durch die Stille braust das Meer
Eintönig um die Stadt.

Es rauscht kein Wald, es schlägt im Mai
Kein Vogel ohn' Unterlaß;
Die Wandergans mit hartem Schrei
Nur fliegt in Herbstesnacht vorbei,
Am Strande weht das Gras.

Doch hängt mein ganzes Herz an dir,
Du graue Stadt am Meer;
Der Jugend Zauber für und für
Ruht lächelnd doch auf dir, auf dir,
Du graue Stadt am Meer.

My ornate "The Town" is an elaborate variation on Storm's theme, with only superficial resemblance to the stark simplicity of the original.

THE TOWN

Monochrome sea, gray drizzly spray,
       and a town, the colour of slate,
where gables bend in slow degrees
under the fog's spectral weight,
and on the strand in briny breeze
       marsh-grasses sway.

No woods nearby. No birds to sing in May.
No glint of spring. Sunlight remains a hint,
       by June it fades away.
The humid August air stays warm.
The town — damp, desolate, forlorn.
       The clouds look torn.
Harsh cries of passing waterfowl
pierce through the chilly gloom of fall,
       the days grow small.

Yet all my heart belongs to you,
fog-ridden town,
       monochrome
squatter behind the frothy foam,
birdless, cheerless, monotonous
tenant of the North Sea:
       You own
me, all magic is yours alone,

because no other petty truth
matches the miracle of youth,
gray town!
                 Wild geese and misty strand,
for all your marsh-grassy desolation,
sun-deprived vistas, briny smells,
you are my self-defining station
of Calvary, my inspiration,
homeland, memory, elation:
Was I a child anywhere else?

When rendering "*Abends*" into English, I managed to remain somewhat more faithful to Storm's actual words and structure.

EVENING

Why do violets exude a denser redolence at night?
Why do waiting lips blush crimson, as if set alight, at night?
Why does a profound desire stir in my delighted heart
at the thought of kissing blushing burning crimson lips at night?

ABENDS

Warum duften die Levkojen soviel schöner bei der Nacht?
Warum brennen deine Lippen soviel röter bei der Nacht?
Warum ist in meinem Herzen so die Sehnsucht
auferwacht,
Diese brennend roten Lippen dir zu küssen bei der Nacht?

Storm's title for the third poem is *"Beginn des Endes."* This sounded a little too Churchillian for three short stanzas, even three stanzas about cardiac matters, so I decided to call my English version "Wild Card." I have taken a few other liberties, but left the heart of the poem (as it were) unchanged.

WILD CARD

It's a shuffle, devoid of pain,
a feeling, dim and passing.
Yet there, it interrupts again …
Altogether surpassing

nuisance! What can it be? Nothing,
too amorphous, too slight to rate.
Skipping stone in the chest. A sting,
hard to describe, harder to shake.

How curious, the lamps turn black.
And suddenly you know. A card,
dealt from the bottom of the deck,
death's hand, brushing against your heart.

Radnóti

LET US REGRESS FROM the nineteenth to the twentieth century. Miklós Radnóti was born in the spring of 1909, and executed by fascist militiamen in the fall of 1944. His last poems were found in a notebook in his coat pocket after his body was exhumed from a mass grave near a village in north-western Hungary. The four short "Postcards," included in this collection, were the final entries.

POSTCARDS FROM SERBIA
(August 30, 1944–October 31, 1944)

1.
Across the mountain ridge, from Bulgaria,
a dense artillery barrage, war's feral aria
broke over men, horses, hopes, jammed up on the plain;
the savage road bucked, the sky shook its mane.
In this bedlam, in a world run amok,
as motionless and silent as a rock,
like a lodestar shining over destruction, you stood.
Or like an insect burrowing deep into wood.

2.

Six miles distant, houses and haystacks
smoulder.
Cinders swirl on the road. Uneasy rustics
shuffle along the shoulder.
On this side of the war, driving her flock to water,
a barefoot shepherd lass
steps in the glassy pond. Slurping clouds from the surface,
her sheep ripple the glass.

3.

Bloody drool trickles from the oxen in their traces,
the ditch is dotted with piles of bloody feces,
blood is knotted in the company's bootlaces,
disgusting death is breathing in their faces.

4.

I dropped beside him, his body flipped over,
taut as a snapping string, flicking mud in my ear.
Headshot. "A round in the back of the neck,"
I told myself. "Lie still, your turn is near."
The fruit of patience, death, follows the pain.
"He still wriggles," a voice called out in German,
then added something no longer germane.

The gifted poet and translator came from a Jewish family
named Glatter. Being Jewish was rarely an advantage in history,

but it was particularly inadvisable in Nazi-occupied Europe. Radnóti's late conversion to Catholicism in 1943 did nothing to save his life, and was probably not even motivated by an attempt to do so — at least not solely. The exhausted and starving man, shot to death by the escort during the forced march of his labour squadron's retreat from the pursuing Red Army, was a thoroughly assimilated Hungarian patriot. In terms of ethnic or religious self-identification, he did not have a Jewish bone in his body. He devoted his life to his native country's culture, and died bequeathing the last pearls of his talent to the language and literature of the swine that murdered him.

Radnóti's death came about eight months before V-E day. He was thirty-five — much too young to die for anyone except, possibly, a poet. Although his best poems were probably still unwritten, Radnóti left behind a substantial legacy, which included some memorable love lyrics to his extremely pretty wife, Fanni. In this limited sense, at least, the pursuit of poetry is rewarding. There are few occupations in which Radnóti could have achieved as much in so short a time.

One of the most gifted Hungarians to perish in the Holocaust is represented in this volume by two poems. "Postcards" and "Columbus" (to follow) are free, though not fanciful, translations.

COLUMBUS

October twenty-one. A breezy day.
Enters the sound. The shallows fall away.
There's India. No reason to delay.
He picks his cautious path along the bay.

Smearing honey on his sun-cankered lips
Watches the green monkeys eye his ships
Hanging from trees by prehensile tails.
They wait to see if he succeeds or fails.

He begged and lied. He attended masses.
Waited in ante-rooms. Mounted royal asses.
Received succour. Did not return pity.
Now he's sailing into eternity.

Fresh fruit and timber and his ships at anchor,
Serene in victory, no rivals, rancor,
Prays briefly to Christ he feigns to adore.
His smelly sailors follow him ashore.

He is tired. His eyelids are burning.
The hills are still. The cobalt waves are churning.
And on the brink of a life everlasting
He turns around. And says something in passing.

Pushkin

THE CLASSICIST RADNÓTI WOULD have preferred to dodge the bullet that killed him. The romantic Pushkin, born a hundred and ten years earlier, went out of his way to run into one.

FREEDOM'S MERCENARY

Battle, I think we've met ... Sabre, your rattle
is music ... Think of my house as home ...
Welcome, dear war. Skeletal skull and bone,
spirit of extinction, fond friend! Test my mettle,
invite me, pray, to stare down death, to serve,
to offer liberty a hand. A pleasant duty.
Whoever ignores it, doesn't know or deserve
the bliss of her kiss, the caress of her beauty.

In the shared view of the reading public and the canons of official literary criticism, Aleksandr Sergeyevich Pushkin is the greatest poet in the Russian language. It is a view from which I will not dissent, noting only that lesser poets often write individual poems that are as beautiful as any written by giants like Pushkin.

Born in 1799, the progenitor of modern Russian literature started publishing poetry as a teenager, and was acknowledged as a major talent from the start. As an entertainer he was coddled by the court and the authorities who felt both amused and annoyed by the Byronic airs of the great-grandson of Peter the Great's "blackamoor" protégée, Ibrahim Petrovich Gannibal, a courtier of note himself three generations earlier. Being admired and at the same time resented, Pushkin was shunted back and forth between triumph and humiliation, court life and exile; between rank and perquisites as a poet, and punishment and ostracism as a radical and a social reformer. His wife, the enticing and flirtatious Natalya Goncharova, attracted the attention of the Czar himself — a mixed blessing, under the circumstances, that eventually led to a duel, not between the poet and his sovereign, of course, but between Pushkin and the adopted son of the Dutch ambassador, Georges-Charles de Heeckeren d'Anthès, who had just married Natalya's sister. "But why?" you might ask. Don't. The intrigue was complex enough to form the basis of several literary works, including my stage play *Pushkin* that had a brief run at Toronto's St. Lawrence Centre in the spring of 1979. Suffice it to say that in the ensuing shootout at dawn in the winter of 1837 Russia's greatest poet, the author of *Boris Godunov*, *The Queen of Spades*, *Ruslan and Lyudmila*, and *Eugene Onegin*, fell mortally wounded, having provoked his new French brother-in-law to shoot him for no reason at all.

Pushkin's works are widely available in English. I'm offering the merest taste of his poetry here in the free translation of two short poems. "Rebirth" (below) is free enough, and "Freedom's Mercenary" is even freer.

REBIRTH

Some feckless, slipshod dilettante
couldn't begin to comprehend
genius, and over-daubed
the masterpiece with heavy hand.

But long years crack the cheap veneer,
the false paint peels, and a splash
of light cleanses the canvas as
blood tints the painted figures' flesh.

So falls our soul's grim grime away
to show in sunset's dying rays
the vital vision of our first,
our formative, our sacred days.

Nekrasov

NIKOLAI ALEXEYVICH NEKRASOV WAS born twenty-two years
after Pushkin and seven years after Lermontov. He was the third
member of the poetic triumvirate that ruled Russian literature
in the nineteenth century. Perhaps the least lyrically gifted of the
three, he had the most highly developed social conscience. He
was also the most familiar with life outside court circles and the
army — Lermontov and Pushkin knew little else — as well as with
the art, craft, and business of literature, making his mark as an
editor, publisher, and critic in addition to being a writer of verse.

Living to what for a Russian romantic poet was the ripe old
age of fifty-seven — he died in 1878 — Nekrasov had time to
explore some feelings and emotions associated with adulthood,
tempering the somewhat adolescent tone that characterizes his
peers of the period. Eulogized by Dostoyevsky as Russia's greatest
after Pushkin and Lermontov, the author of *Who is Happy in
Russia?* came from a family of small nobility: a Russian father he
hated and a Polish mother he loved. My offering in this collection
is the free translation of one of his autobiographical poems.

MY FATHER'S HOUSE

Home, home again, where my vile ancestors,
rotten, rambunctious, base, like rooting hogs,
trampled decency underfoot and, sated,
wallowed in their own filth, then fêted
themselves all over, slept, broke wind, and waited
for the next round. Their serfs envied the dogs.
I was born here, oh yes; and as a child
I learned to be miserable and wild,
to dress up hate in the garb of charm,
how to be venomous; how to disarm,
to be unmanageable and how to manage;
to be a landowner, an autocrat,
to shed innocence, and how to capture
a speck of gold: bliss from the dross of rapture.
Oh yes; childhood for others recalls Eden,
forbidden fruit perhaps, affection, freedom:
ah, birch trees, shades of youth. I do not miss them,
memories shame and chill me as I list them …

The park looms dark. Behind the hedges, who
is that anxious, sickly face, but you.
Oh, I knew why you wept, Mother. I knew
who kept your heart an open wound; I knew
how he did it, senseless and crude,

hurling abuse, a rude barbarian,
and I also knew exactly when
the petty despot made you cry.
The only thing I did not know was why,
or why you suffered to remain his slave
for which he chose to hound you to your grave,
and you, to forgive him with your final sigh.

Another woman shared my mother's fate.
Seeking to escape her home, my late
sister bravely forced the doors
of the tyrant's prison of low louts and whores
only to reach a new house of grief, where she,
fleeing the devil, drowned in the deep blue sea.
My mother's peer in torture, pride, and carriage,
uncomplaining, coped with a loveless marriage,
then on her bier, with grief and grace so fierce
she lay, it drove her murderer to tears …

The empty house is falling down. No chorus
of servants, hunters, gamblers, bawling whores,
no sound of breaking glass, carousing lout …
Nightmare necklace, the naked rooms string out.
Memories! Through this hallway I ran crying
to nurse, a kindly, gentle soul, forever trying
to console and sooth. She reassured, she cheered,
she calmed me down, turned everything I feared
into something small … Oh, how I grieved for her,

tears of respect and gratitude. No more,
when I recall her now my heart is cool:
she turned me into a lesser man, the fool.
Never cherish good, simple people. They will
cause grievous harm by making small of evil,
counseling cheer, believing it suffices …
Oh house of birth, the seed of all my vices!

Dry disgust parches me. One thing slakes it: decay.
The old arbour is gone. Blackened stumps show where they
amputated the trees. It vanished, too, the birch,
on which woodpigeons used to perch.
The river runs no more. Cracks in the clay.
Dust rises from the fields. The flocks? Wandered away.
In slow, steady collapse, the house: a faint echo
of sobs and clinking glasses, it sags beneath the snow —
or sags beneath his sins, this pile of peeling plaster,
of one who used to be its proud, unbending master.

Babits

THE LORD'S PRAYER, 1914

Lord, our Father in heaven,
thy struggling, sinning, filth-ridden,
orphaned people call. Pray, listen.
O hallowed be thy sacred name,
God, who art peace. The same.
Thy kingdom come.
Our country bleeds, we are at war,
thy hand's terrible weight we fear
and say anxiously, set to flee:
Thy will be done —
grant us to say it easily,
celestially, all as one.
Thy tree-defending godly soul
prunes boughs for the good of the whole.
But is not, yet, at every turn,

the smallest twig protected by
thy gravest fatherly concern
on earth, as it is in heaven?
Thou couldst not have been more severe.
Having shaken us to the roots,
spare us some leaves until the fall:
give us this day our daily bread.
And teach our children peace. Our feet
slip in blood for their sake, we think,
thy proud creation's weakest link.
Have mercy on our orphaned lasses.
And forgive us our trespasses,
as we forgive those who trespass
against us. We pray at Mass:
vengeance is thine, to punish evil,
ours is to but to shield the nation.
And lead us not into temptation,
so that a sense of innocence
may, like full armour, cover us
and splattered though it is with blood
no feeble doubt may penetrate.
Woe to those who move against us,
the foe cannot gain thy people,
but deliver us from evil:
thine is the kingdom, and its fate
is in thy hands. So is our faith
that those who do confess thy name,
having survived thy gory wrath,

will by thy gentle grace attain

soon, at the far shore of pain,

the power and the glory yet.

MIHÁLY BABITS WAS PROBABLY the most influential literary figure of the era associated with the periodical *Nyugat* (*The West*), which in turn was probably the most influential publication in the history of Hungarian literature. *Nyugat* first appeared in 1908, when Babits was twenty-five, and its last issue was printed in 1941, the year of Babits's death. Between those dates "the power and the glory" (to borrow a line from his poem in this book) belonged to Babits and his fellow contributors to *Nyugat*. Arguably, the early part of this period also coincided with the high water mark of Hungary's civilization.

Born of a good family in the wine-country seat of Szekszárd in 1883, Babits read Hungarian, French, and Latin philology at the University of Budapest. After graduating in 1905, he began teaching and writing poetry, which is essentially what he did for the rest of his life. All that happened after the publication of his first book in 1909 was that his audience grew steadily along with his reputation.

It was a reputation well deserved. Babits and his peers, the so-called "first-generation" contributors to *Nyugat* — notably Ady, Juhász, Kosztolányi, and Tóth — were undoubtedly the most gifted of all poets and translators in a culture that was rich in the tradition of poetry. What the first generation was less likely to acknowledge was that some members of the generation following on their heels — notably Attila József, Miklós Radnóti, or Lörinc Szabó — were probably their peers.

Babits especially had difficulty accepting that the mentally unstable son of an itinerant soap-maker and a washerwoman, Attila József, could be his equal as a poet. As editor of *Nyugat* after 1916, it was up to him when to publish the impoverished genius. He rarely did. After József laid his right arm on a railroad track and died in 1937, another poet, George Faludy, then twenty-seven, wrote that "the wheel of the train was no harder than Mihály Babits's heart." It was an intemperate thing to say about a literary icon and great pacifist poet, but under the circumstances not altogether inaccurate.

Babits died four years later in Budapest, at fifty-eight, of throat cancer. His poetry survives. Probably his most frequently quoted line is from his epic, *The Book of Jonas* (The Old Testament prophet — no relation to the author): "... *vétkesek közt cinkos, aki néma.*" It could be rendered as "... those who stand mute are accomplices to evil." It was the poet's judgment on his generation and perhaps on himself as well.

"The Lord's Prayer, 1914," is as close to being a free translation of Babits' original as any poem in this book. How close is that? Those who read Hungarian may judge for themselves.

MIATYÁNK 1914

Miatyánk ki vagy a mennyekben
harcokban, bűnökben, szennyekben,
rád tekint árva világod:
a te neved megszenteltessék,
a te legszebb neved: Békesség!
Jöjjön el a te országod.
Véres a földünk, háború van,
kezed sujtását sejtjük, uram,
s mondjuk, de nyögve, szomorúan,
add, hogy mondhassuk könnyebben --:
Legyen meg a te akaratod!
mint angyalok mondják mennyekben.
Előtted uram, a hon java,
s hulljon a lomb, csak éljen a fa:
de vajon a legkisebb lombot
nem őrzi-e atyai gondod?
nem leng-e az utolsó fürtön is
áldva miképpen mennyekben,
azonképpen itt a földön is?
Megráztál, nem lehet szörnyebben,
már most ami fánkon megmaradt
őrizd meg őszig a bús gallyat:
mindennapi kenyerünket add
meg nekünk ma, és gyermekeinket
növeld békére: ha bűn, hogy lábunk
ma vérbe csúszik meg: értük az!

Bocsásd meg a mi bűneinket,
miképpen mi is megbocsátunk
ellenünk vétetteknek: a gaz
tied, büntetni: mienk csak az,
hogy védelmezzük a mieinket!
És ne vigy a kísértetbe minket,
hogy ártatlanságunk tudatát,
mint drága páncélos inget
őrizzük meg bár véresen,
hogy át ne hasadjon sohasem.
Jaj, aki ellenünk mozdul:
megvívunk, készen, bármi csatát,
de szabadíts meg a gonosztul,
mert tiéd az ország,
kezedbe tette le sorsát,
s te vagy a legnagyobb erősség:
ki neveden buzdul,
bármennyit küzd és vérez,
előbb vagy utóbb övé lesz
a hatalom és a dicsőség.

Jammes

IT IS MY CONTENTION that so-called minor poets write some of the most beautiful poems. Here is one from early twentieth-century France:

WHITE ROSES IN THE AFTERNOON

White roses in the afternoon, wilting in torpid clusters,
the raspy buzz of wasps, zig-zagging in the rafters,
the indolent boom of bells, announcing vespers;
the grapes, transparent stones, talking in whispers,
bunched up in the gazebo, sleepy drifters:
In this house I could love you. My entire,
bold, 24-year-old, white-rose scented ouvre
is yours, my mocking poetry, my daring lyre.
Yet I have never met you. All my dire
need is for naught because you have not bothered
to be born. You are a creature I fathered
to live with me, and if you did live, you would.

On sweltering days we'd saunter through the woods
where ash leaves touch, arches stretch alabaster,
boiling sun hisses, and yellow insects dance.
Our tightly welded kisses would dissolve in laughter
as in the red aftertaste of your lips
roses mingled with sweet grapes and the venom of the wasps.

Francis Jammes had a relatively long life for a poet, perhaps as a consolation from Fate for not making him fashionable enough to be elected to the "immortals" of the *Académie française*. Born in 1868, he died at seventy just a year before the outbreak of World War II. A provincial, indeed rural, lyricist, he remained something of an outsider in the literary salons of Paris. This did not stop him from writing many exquisite and imaginative poems, nor in acquiring enough of an audience to live on his income as a poet and writer — which was more than some of the "immortals" could say.

The poem in this collection (above) is my variation on a theme by Jammes, but it borrows enough of the French poet's cadences and imagery to pass for a free translation — which is the claim I'm making for it.

Vajda

JÁNOS VAJDA (1827–1897) WAS another minor poet who wrote a few major poems, one of which follows in my free but not unfaithful translation:

TWENTY YEARS LATER

Like ice at the summit of Mont Blanc,
there is no sun, no crucible
to melt it. It's not possible.
My heart is passion-free. A blank.

Around it billions of stars
flash flirtatiously, twirl and dart,
gleam Venus-blue, glow red like Mars:
nothing ignites my icy heart.

Sometimes, though, in the dead of night,
a dreamscape rises up, a sight:
on the lake of my youth, a swan,
a moment only. Then you're gone.

At such times my heart briefly glows
as, at the dawn of frosty days,
the rising sun's rhapsodic rays
light up Mont Blanc's eternal snows.

"Twenty Years Later" is from the Gina-cycles of love poems, written over a period of nearly forty years, between 1854 and 1892. It is probably Vajda's most anthologized piece; at least, I have not seen any collection of nineteenth-century Hungarian poetry without it.

A handsome young poet and itinerant actor, Vajda grew into a sickly and cranky old codger. He married for the first time at age fifty-three, choosing a bride of nineteen, Rozália Bartos, but threw her out of the house two years later on discovering that the young girl had "a past." She might have been lucky. Vajda spent the remaining fifteen years of his life in poverty and alone.

Várady

SZABOLCS VÁRADY WAS BORN in Budapest in 1943. He is the only poet in this collection who is alive. (George Faludy was still alive when I started this book.)

I know next to nothing about Várady's poetry. I saw "Precautions" in an anthology, liked it, and translated it (well, more or less). When I looked up the author afterwards, I discovered that he had not only won a string of major poetry awards since the 1980s, but spent a year in the USA as a Fulbright scholar, was at one time senior editor of the Anglo-American section of a Budapest publisher, and could probably have done a better job rendering his poem into English than I did.

PRECAUTIONS

I take certain precautions with the dead.
They aren't. Do they know it? Hard to tell.
As you enter the room, you say hello.
Spectres rarely do, and never say it well.
Still, you seem no less bashful than I am.
We play a game "as if" first. Then we fuss,
like intensive care visitor and patient,
trying to be credibly credulous.

How much time have you left? How much have I?
You do not guess. You kiss. Your lips are candid.
You never mimic longing: you are, ergo you long.
It would be paltry to misunderstand it.
We stand forlorn. The snowflakes whirl around us.
The sun's not up yet. It's so cold it pains.
I love you. You said that once: I love you.
The snow melted, they piled some earth above you,
this much remains.

Rilke

AS I WAS PILOTING a small plane on a hot summer day from
Toronto to Windsor, the drone of the engine insisted on repeating
the opening words of *Herbsttag*, one of Rilke's frequently antholo-
gized poems. *Herr-es-ist-Zeit, Herr-es-ist-Zeit* … By the time I
landed in the sweltering Canadian border town across the river
from Detroit, the four-cylinder Lycoming aero-engine had trans-
lated Autumn Day's twelve lines into English and fixed them
firmly in my mind. Once safely on the tarmac, I wrote them in
the logbook.

AUTUMN DAY

Lord: It is time. The summer was fair.
Rest your shadow on the sundial's face,
Release the autumn breezes in the air.
Order the last grapes to ripen on the vine,

Let them have two more southerly days
As sunlight shimmers, morning frost delays,
And the seed's sweetness yields a weighty wine.

Who is now homeless, will never build a home.
He'll roam in rooms inside a stranger's house,
Wake with a start, write long letters, and browse
In brittle books, then in alleys alone,
Watch the curling leaves whirl without a pause.

Rainer Maria Rilke is usually referred to only by his last name. Born and raised in the Czech or, more precisely, Bohemian city of Prague; culturally German, and by citizenship Austro-Hungarian, the leading trans-national poet of the nineteenth-cum-twentieth century lived for various parts of his life in Russia, Italy, France, and Switzerland. The first two-thirds of his passage — he was born in 1875 and died in 1926 — came at the tail end of the most civilized, passport-free period of Victorian-Edwardian Europe.

Though working mainly in German, Rilke did compose some poems in French, and would be remembered for his achievement in that language alone. His sexual life was as ambiguous as his literary and linguistic leanings, and he required a fair amount of emotional, existential, material, medical, and practical support. Like many other poets, Rilke could be counted on for a calamity a day, ranging from an administrative hitch to some crisis of heart, conscience, or creativity, making him something of a pain in the neck.

He was well worth the trouble, of course, certainly from a reader's point of view — but then a good writer is always a bargain for a reader whose sole cost is the price of his/her book. Friends, lovers, family, agents, publishers, editors, even acquaintances and tradesmen, pay more. But fragile as Rilke may have been, he was also sufficiently rewarding never to lack patrons and supporters. His attachments, though unconventional, were usually long-lasting — for example, to the wealthy bluestocking Lou Andreas-Salome, or to the sculptor, Clara Westhoff, whom he married, or to the painter, Lou Albert-Lasard, whom he did not. He died in a Swiss sanatorium, of leukemia, at the age of fifty-one.

My "Autumn Day" is faithful enough to pass for a free translation; "Apollo's Archaic Torso" (below) is my variation on Rilke's theme — with the apple remaining, I think, in the general vicinity of the tree. The interested reader may wish to look at the original first:

ARCHAÏSCHER TORSO APOLLOS

Wir kannten nicht sein unerhörtes Haupt,
darin die Augenäpfel reiften. Aber
sein Torso glüht noch wie ein Kandelaber,
in dem sein Schauen, nur zurückgeschraubt,

sich hält und glänzt. Sonst könnte nicht der Bug
der Brust dich blenden, und im leisen Drehen

der Lenden könnte nicht ein Lächeln gehen
zu jener Mitte, die die Zeugung trug.

Sonst stünde dieser Stein entstellt und kurz
unter der Schultern durchsichtigem Sturz
und flimmerte nicht so wie Raubtierfelle

und bräche nicht aus allen seinen Rändern
aus wie ein Stern: denn da ist keine Stelle
die dich nicht sieht. Du musst dein Leben ändern.

And this is the way I hear it in English:

APOLLO'S ARCHAIC TORSO

One wonders if the unknowable eyes
were molten cores like magma, set to scorch
spectators with their blazing gaze. A torch,
the headless torso glows as it replies

with high-vaulted marble chest to dazzle
above the flying buttress of the hips
and procreative centre to eclipse
what it has posited, an ancient puzzle.

Without this, nothing. Merely broken stone,
a pair of undistinguished shoulders, prone
to drooping — and no predator's pelt, rife

with coruscating feral tiger-lights,
flashes that sear and fix you in their sights,
like rays reversed. You must remake your life.

Rilke's influence on modern literature and, to a lesser extent, philosophy and art criticism, was tremendous. Canada's defining expression, the title of Hugh MacLennan's 1945 novel, *Two Solitudes*, comes from Rilke's "Letters to a Young Poet": *Love consists in this, / that two solitudes protect, / and touch, and greet each other*. He is translated into English very widely, and the two poems selected for this collection have been particularly popular. There was no crying need to offer either in a new English version, but my Lycoming engine felt like it, and so did I.

Kosztolányi

BORN IN 1885, TO a small-town family of pharmacists and "seven plum-tree" gentry (a reference to the size of the ancestral estate) the first year of the twentieth century saw Dezső Kosztolányi turn sixteen. He celebrated it by publishing his first poem. At nineteen he started reading arts at the universities of Vienna and Budapest, but interrupted his studies at twenty-one to accept an editorship at the periodical *Budapesti Napló (Budapest Diaries)* which had printed his first poem five years earlier. He was twenty-three when his byline appeared in *Nyugat (The West),* the leading literary journal of his generation, and within a short time he became an important and frequent contributor, ranking with such luminaries of Hungarian modernity as Endre Ady, Mihály Babits, and Árpád Tóth. While not a child prodigy or even unusually precocious for a lyric poet, Kosztolányi seemed to spring on stage "in full armour," like Pallas Athena from Zeus's head. Remembered primarily as a poet and translator today, he was also a remarkable short story writer, a gifted essayist, accomplished editor, and the author of two of the finest short novels in Hungarian literature: *Pacsirta (Skylark)* and *Édes Anna (Sweet Anna).*

In this collection, "I'm On File …" and "Eulogy" are free translations of Kosztolányi's well-known poems. "Ottawa" is a make-believe postcard written in his manner.

I'M ON FILE …

I'm on file in offices of all sorts
catalogued and archived in their books.
In dusty ledgers I, too, am an entry
for clerks to list, staple, or overlook.
O gnashing teeth! The humiliation!
To be confined to some accountant's cage,
and condemned to make my name the sentry
over my own prison on a page.
I would much rather rot beneath the compost,
or, howling like a sandstorm, run amok,
than — reduced to data — languish unfree,
catalogued and filed in dusty books.

EULOGY

Dearly beloved, he decided to leave us
and by departing, deprive and deceive us.
We knew him, not as a monument in stone,
but as a dear heart, akin to our own.
As he reposes,
alas, his measure lapses.
His account closes.
The treasury collapses.

Let us learn from his lesson. He was lonely,
a sole copy, another one-and-only.
More of him never have been, never will be,
in ten million light years he will still be
unique as a drawing, or a bird in motion,
a tune, a meteor, a fingerprint, an ocean.
Look at him lying there. The hand and wrist
stretch into ineluctable mist,
a heraldic device,
frozen in ice,
carved in hieroglyphs, like a sacred
relic, his matchless life's eternal secret.

He was the lock and he was the passkey.
Whoever he might have been, he was he.
The way he preferred one dish to another,

the nickname by which he referred to his lover,
or how he cursed his favorite appliance
before his lips were sternly sealed by silence;
or how his voice rang out recently: "Miss, please,
will you cut for me a bit of Swiss cheese?"
How he drank harsh wine, or whispered: "Let's elope,"
or watched the slowly undulating smoke
from a cheap cigarette between his fingers
whose odour in his living room still lingers,
or how he dreamt, telephoned, carried on,
all stamped him as unique — and now he is gone.

He had no peer in creation. Berlin, Alsace-Lorraine,
Asia or the moon: you look for him in vain.
Lost to the past, the future hasn't got him,
anyone may yet be born — but not him.
By his casket two of his portraits post guards:
coming from the far shore, they're only postcards.
Our grief is rich enough to miss or berate him,
fortune herself too poor to recreate him.

Dear friends, behold the fairy tale's hero,
whose chances for coming to life were zero
until it pleased destiny to shape him
so we could smugly begin to narrate him:

"Once upon a time …" before his existence
was rudely cut short without going the distance.
He dabbled in art, the history of culture,
now he lies as his own glaciated sculpture,
later to vaporize like a wave that crested,
disposable, not to be resurrected.

It's more civilized to pacify evil
than to erase, blow up, or throttle it;
cultivating peace as Niagara's ice wine,
our great north hopes to grow and bottle it.
But bringing wine to market is a delicate task.
In vintage vineyards people used to say
"Drink it from a flask but age it in a cask."
Peace is the same. It ages no better
than some wines do, inside a bottle.
Siphoned too soon, it matures for an hour,
then, instead of becoming robust or subtle,
it turns sour.

Kosztolányi was immensely attractive both as a writer and
as a person. Like Verdi, he did not want to quarrel with the
audience — nor was he particularly anxious to please it. He
wanted to please the artist in himself. His style created the initial
impression that he would dazzle readers rather than move them,
but he was eminently capable of doing both, and did. Though
his palette had many dark tones, as a human being he seemed
mercifully free of the inner and outer turmoil that is often the
concomitant of major (or even minor) talent. He revealed himself
early, was recognized rapidly, and as a liberal-minded Edwardian
gentleman from a "good" — but not wealthy — family, he fit into
his particular segment of Hungary's multi-layered society with

ease. Liked and respected by his readers as well as his peers, at the age of forty-five he became president of the Hungarian PEN club. Six years later, in 1936, he died of cancer, which — in Attila József's words — was gnawing at him much like emerging monster states were gnawing at humanity.

Now Kosztolányi is gone, and so are the monster states of his day. New monster states have emerged, and so have new poets. Humanity is hanging on.

Tóth

ÁRPÁD TÓTH (1886-1928) was the fourth prominent member of the *Nyugat* (*The West*) generation of poets in Hungary, along with Ady, Babits, and Kosztolányi. Bridging modernity and post-modernity, rooted in the *fin de siècle* but doing the bulk of their work in the first half of the twentieth century, these poets shared a quality of technical brilliance, finely honed erudition, and a more or less elegiac temper — all except Ady, whose temper was anything but elegiac, although he sometimes laid claim to feelings of resigned sadness. What was at most a pose in Ady, however, was second nature in Tóth. His are poems of intricately orchestrated, melodious, highly polished grief.

A provincial artist's son (Tóth's father was a failed sculptor in the agricultural town of Debrecen), he preferred literature to life — not surprisingly, for he was much better at it. As a man he was a mere whisper: he barely lasted forty-two years before tuberculosis carried him off; as a superb translator and poet, his voice is still heard in the twenty-first century. In this collection he is represented only by my attempt at a free translation of his midget masterpiece about a discarded matchstick.

FLAME

I threw away a match, which promptly
burst into a fiery romp: he
stood on tiptoes, became a lean,
vivacious yellow flame, a keen
conspirator, who wanted,
with a confidence unwarranted,
to be a match unmatched: a spry
force to illuminate the sky,
igniting in his heart the ardour
required to burn down the arbour.
But huge trees, haughty and sterile,
ignored the perky flame's peril.
The flowers smiled. Even the grass
Dismissed his sally as mere brass.
The midget flame, his fever spent,
grew tired and sat. Sensed the end.
Flared once more, gave a fizzling sigh,
then lay on the forest's floor to die.

Nobody witnessed it but I.

A reader might object that the word "sterile" cannot possibly
be the *mot juste* to describe a living thing and I have chosen it
just for the sake of the rhyme. It is true that I chose "sterile"
because it rhymes with "peril," but resistance to catching the

firebug is a form of sterility, which makes it a fair use. This is the kind of flexibility that allows language to be so much fun when embraced by poets, and so dangerous when twisted by lawyers and demagogues. This is a subject for another day.

Faludy

THE ONLY PERSONAL FRIEND in these pages — indeed, the only poet in this book I actually knew — was George (György) Faludy. For this reason, my thumbnail sketch about him will be slightly longer.

Born in 1910, Faludy belonged to the generation that preceded mine. I came to regard him as my teacher, for which he was in no way responsible. The poet never reached out to make me, or (as far as I know) anyone else, his disciple. When he did reach out, as he did from time to time, it was to make aesthetic, political, or sometimes sexual gestures. Other than recounting fables disguised as true stories, or true stories disguised as fables, Faludy did little but write and recite poems. He told his tales in cafés, parks, ditches, prison cells, over whatever loaves of bread and jugs of wine happened to be available to him. A showman, not an educator, he did lecture at various universities from time to time, but for the performance rather than for the fee, let alone out of a sense of vocation as a teacher. He accepted financial assistance graciously, but never asked for any. He was usually broke.

In Hungary, where he is a household name, Faludy never spent twenty consecutive years. In Canada, where he lived from 1967 until 1989, few people have heard of him. In Hungary, he was a national icon, a poet of the people, though noticed only condescendingly, if at all, by the tin-eared eunuchs of the literary establishment. In the West, it was the opposite. Faludy was a delicacy for the cognoscenti, the elect who knew his poetry or his autobiography, *My Happy Days in Hell.* Universities gave him honorary doctorates, and his works were translated, reviewed, edited, prefaced, and published by such literary and journalistic figures as Arnold Toynbee, George Mikes, Arthur Koestler, and Andre Deutsch in Britain, or Raymond Souster, Robin Skelton, Gwendolyn MacEwan, Dennis Lee, Nick Harris, John Robert Colombo, and Barbara Amiel in Canada.

He burst onto the literary scene in the 1930s with a slim volume of brash poems written in the manner of François Villon. His verses were erotic and coruscating. They were also subversive, militantly anti-fascist, and offensive to Hungary's German allies. The Hungarian authorities, well right-of-centre but still semi-civilized, gave him a choice between arrest and exile. Faludy chose Paris. He had barely arrived there when the war broke out. Faludy and his then-wife, Vali Ács, fled the invading Nazis, making their way first to Morocco, then, on President Roosevelt's invitation, to America. Faludy enlisted in the U.S. Air Force and saw service in the Pacific as a tail gunner (at least, according to some of his war stories). Showing more optimism than foresight, he returned to Hungary after the war, where he was soon arrested by the Communist regime and taken to the infamous stone quarries of Recsk. He survived and was released after Stalin's death in 1953.

I was first introduced to the poet in Budapest's gilded literary local, the New York Café, shortly after his discharge from the labour camp. A cabaret-writer friend named Potyó took me to the table of a swarthy man in his mid-forties with large, dark, impish eyes and a mischievous smile. At nineteen, I knew many of his poems by heart. An older friend, a boy who already shaved, had lent me Faludy's book when I was about fourteen. This must have been around the time the fabulist-author, being interrogated in the cellars of the Communist secret police, broke down and confessed that he was an American spy, having been recruited by Captain Walt Whitman and Lieutenant Edgar Allan Poe of the U.S. Office of Strategic Services. The mockery would entail little risk: Stalin's sadistic henchmen in Hungary were illiterate.

The tattered paperback of Villon's poetry was a revelation. I had read poetry before — in my school everyone had to — but only for class assignments, and without much enjoyment. Faludy changed that. His variations on Villon became the first poems I ever read of my own volition. By the time I was offered a seat at his table in 1954, I had published one or two poems myself.

Following the defeat of the Hungarian revolution of 1956, Walt Whitman and Edgar Allan Poe's man in Budapest fled to Austria with his second wife, Zsuzsa Szegö, an ethereal ex-Communist blonde. It was Zsuzsa, working as a translator for the Canadian Legation in Vienna, who facilitated my visa to Canada a few weeks later.

The poet was nearly fifty when he settled in London to sum up his eventful life in a scintillating autobiography. In an excellent English translation by Kathleen Szász (who, according to Faludy, never liked him) *My Happy Days in Hell* produced acclaim, plus an unexpected side effect. His name was Eric.

Eric the Erotic, as I nicknamed him, although he seemed erotic to me only when viewed through Faludy's eyes, was an American ballet dancer. Old enough to have served as a U.S. Army intelligence clerk in Korea, but still only twenty-six when Faludy's book appeared, Eric Johnson read the American edition and became obsessed with the idea of meeting the man who wrote it.

He found him in Malta, where Faludy, by then fifty-six, was living alone following Zsuzsa's untimely death of cancer. As a sexual being, Faludy was an omnivore. He was attracted to beauty, youth, and intellect; the gender to which these qualities were attached made little difference to him. Faludy lustily proceeded to convert Johnson's intellectual love into a physical attachment, via the emotional medium of poetry. The outcome was a group of sonnets, among the finest in the Hungarian language.

Faludy and Johnson spent the next thirty-six years together, living in various parts of the world. He and I caught up with each other after the two of them came to Toronto in 1967 to share a small apartment with a pair of free-flying finches at 25 St. Mary Street. Following the collapse of the Soviet empire, the couple moved back to Budapest, where people worshipped Faludy and tolerated Johnson. The post-Communist government assigned a spacious apartment on the east bank of the Danube for their lifetime use — more precisely, for the lifetime use of Hungary's national icon, for Johnson as the poet's "secretary" had no official status.

Johnson's occupancy of the apartment was rescinded in 2002. It was the year Cupid let loose his arrow and hit Faludy straight in the heart. The national icon fell, and fell hard, for a twenty-six-year-old photo model named Fanny Kovács. Cupid's bulls-eye made Johnson, by then sixty-four, possibly the first man in history to be jilted by a ninety-two-year-old lover.

As Fanny and Faludy were getting ready to wed, Johnson joined the Dalai Lama's entourage in India. He wrote letters to friends saying that he was happier than he had ever been. For all I know, it was true. Still, he either committed suicide or at least did not seek treatment after being diagnosed with cancer in the fall of 2004. His funeral pyre was lit in Katmandu.

Within two years, Faludy himself was laid to rest at a near-state funeral, attended by thousands, in Budapest. He was almost ninety-six. Had he lived another month, he could have come to a ceremony at which Toronto's mayor dedicated a tiny park named after him, across the street from the apartment he had shared with Eric at 25 St. Mary Street. His widow, Fanny, attended the unveiling.

Those who debate Faludy's significance in Hungarian letters do so mainly because they cannot debate his popularity. Although officialdom did finally bestow the country's highest literary award, the Kossuth Prize, on the man long crowned Hungary's "poet-king" by the press, influential critics across the political spectrum still often dismiss him as "lightweight," a "libidinous showman," a "cosmopolitan," a "social-democrat" or sometimes simply as a "Jew." Such critics miss the mark by hitting it. Faludy was a libidinous social-democratic cosmopolitan Jewish show-man — and a great poet. He moved with a lightweight's grace and carried a heavyweight's punch.

When it came to the genre of poetic variations inspired by other poems or poets, Faludy was no pioneer. His predecessors, in modern times alone, include W.B. Yeats, Bertolt Brecht, Edward Fitzgerald, Richard Wagner, and many others. But while Faludy did not invent the genre, he had been an early and successful practitioner of it — early by Hungarian, and successful by global standards. His "Faludy-Villon" book of poems has resulted in some fifty editions since its first printing by Officina of Budapest in 1937.

Faludy's influence permeates this book, including the English-language poems I wrote in his manner. None is a translation, strictly speaking, although *The Crossing* is close to being one. In contrast, *Fascist Deputy* is very far away, while the other three are in-between. Faludy still read and approved *The Crossing* as well as *The Letter* and *Ibn Ammar al-Andalus,* early versions of which appeared in my 1993 collection, *The East Wind Blows West.* Whether or not he was merely being polite, I cannot say. One day perhaps he will let me know what he thought of *A Fascist Deputy* and the sonnet, *I Did Recuperate.* I doubt it, though. Death entitles people to keep some things to themselves.

THE CROSSING

Deep ford, steep waterbed,
silent girls cross it
with eyes accusing and sad,
from rocky shores, their clothes
hanging like sheets of lead.

But let the keen brooks turn lean:
with waist-high skirts aloft
and roving eyes, in a dream
girls are golden thighs in silver water
crossing a summer stream.

THE LETTER WITH WHICH WALAFRIDUS STRABO SUBMITTED HIS BOOK ON HORTICULTURE TO GRIMALDUS, THE ABBOT OF ST. GALL, AROUND 830 A.D.

The book my messenger leaves at your gate
is modest for a gift, not in accord
with the merits of a spirit as ornate
as yours, O my father in the Lord.
But it comes from a follower in the faith
who, while lettering these dashes and dots,
can see you in a rock-garden beneath
a small tree bearing yellow apricots
surrounded by the offspring of your soul,
your family, disciples, casting lots
to gather vegetables for your table
-- laid axial to Canis Major's gable —
at which you dine, and draw celestial plots
under the autumn's ornamental glass.
There, in that garden, gentle father, gazing
over the irises and tiger-grass,
advanced in age but in strength still amazing,
untouched by ill-health, sloth, or gluttony,
read — which I boldly send you for appraising —
my brief commentary on botany.
Ponder deeply my modest creation,
tender me about it no lenient lies,
castigate its faults for my edification,

but if it merits some favour in your eyes,
extol its virtues, O voice that fills the land
with tones of ringing brass in major keys,
for which may Christ place in your ancient hand
the olive branch of His eternal peace.

IBN AMMAR AL-ANDALUSI, 1000 A.D.

The parks, the nights, the naked bodies' blur,
the books, fountains, gold coins in his purse,
the olive trees, mosques, minarets; the myrrh,
the honeyed scent of joy without remorse,
his gem-crusted weapons, his jet-black horse.
In pride he wrote this, because it was clear
within the lustrous balustrades of Seville
all worshipped and quoted him, the Grand Vizier:

"I am Ammar. The fame of my verse flies
over the mountains and the western sea
and from the south a desert wind replies,
only a fool is ignorant of me.
A golden lizard on a golden disc,
if I slither from the lewd lips of a boy
into the eager ear of an odalisque
she leaves her master and becomes my toy.
Nor will this change after my body lies
under an obelisk."

He was cheerful and happier than I,
for when on Spanish domes the arabesque
loosened and fell, he never questioned why,
or why people grew flabby and grotesque,
and did not sense the fabric's fading dye
or in his own tunic the broken thread,

the fountains of the city running dry,
he did not taste the filth inside his bread
or see the boys who knew his poems die
or view the burning library with dread.
Brave and clever, he failed to note the fact
that faith's no help, nor wit, courage, nor dagger,
that no philosophy will resurrect
a culture: collapsing is forever.

"To A Fascist Deputy" is my variation on a theme by Faludy, shaped differently but using some of his imagery.

TO A FASCIST DEPUTY

They say you're ageing. The sludge in your veins
has put a chokehold on what some call your heart.
One day, friends will wrap your bloated remains
in your country's flag and place it on a cart,
     a velvet-covered caisson, coarse and crass,
behind which a riderless stallion prances,
followed by raised hats and respectful glances
     from the procession behind the horse's ass
in homage to your political stances
your cortege being oblivious to virtue,
decency, taste, and similar nuances.

Fully licenced to wield a dental drill,
had you been merely keen on making shrill
        noises, you had the perfect instrument.
Rather than hone your teeth on politics
you could have stuck to filling cavities
        but didn't, to your nation's frank lament.
Nor were you content to hunt in the decaying
woods, or stick to harmlessly laying,
        as other gentry did, your serving wench.
Now roadside acacias are swaying
in slender-fingered autumn breezes, playing
the harp of Transdanubia from end to end,
        and scatter your memory, like a stench.

The electioneering grin wiped off your face,
made unblinking by stern death, tightly lipped,
        bony fingers clutching your venom's list,
the apt place for you is inside the crypt.
Your hate-filled soul is at home in your corpse
where in dank darkness it greedily craves
        the glory of the sorcerer's apprentice,
till it enters that circle of Inferno
        where spirits of irredentist bent twist,
while winter winds whistle across your grave's
        snow-smudged contours, you miserable dentist.

Faludy composed the sonnet "I Did Recuperate …" for the Eric-cycle; I wrote the English version for the unveiling of the Faludy-parkette across from 25 St. Mary Street.

I DID RECUPERATE …

I did recuperate, but no cure is final.
Silence is final: the stiff repose
as my cooling clay stretches out one morning,
grey sheets ill covering serrated toes.

Don't linger by the corpse. Unsightly shroud,
death's sulphur breath will turn it ochre soon.
Don't look for me. I am gone. Draw the curtain,
and let deep shadows occupy the room.

Quote, as you did before, the sage Sankara,
postulating a plane of existence
to which our stubborn spirits retire

to meet again in due time and distance.
Listen to Bach, read the Greeks you admire.
Don't throw yourself on my funeral pyre.

Mallarmé

IS THIS THE SOUND of Stéphane Mallarmé (1842–1898) turning in his grave? I have taken great liberties with his anthology piece "Sea Breeze," though of all the poets in this book he should be the one most prepared to forgive me. I say "should be" because with poets you never know. They may not like it when a critic applies their aesthetic theories to their own work.

The French symbolists, of whose school Mallarmé was a charter member, were also known as *les Mardistes* because they met on Tuesdays. Calling someone a *Tuesdayist* in English — to say nothing of a *Dienstager* in German or a *Keddes* in Hungarian — would not sound very impressive. If anything, it would sound comical, confirming Mallarmé's theory that the sound of words matters as much as their meaning, if not more. However, this, like all truths, can be carried to extremes. By the end of the nineteenth century it gave rise to various outlandish trends in the galleries and salons of France where the modernists of the *fin-de-siècle* congregated, including Mallarmé's "sound first, mean later" school of poetry.

The expression is mine, I hasten to add, not Mallarmé's — and in his best work he did not follow his own school. He fused, instead, sound and meaning, which in fact is what poets have tended to do since time immemorial, proving that in aesthetic theory, as in most other matters, the more things change, the more they remain the same.

Mallarmé had much influence over modern literature, but little over his own finances. He worked as a teacher in Paris, and died as he had lived, in modest circumstances, at the age of fifty-six. Today he may be best remembered for having hosted a literary salon every Tuesday for the likes of Verlaine, Rilke, and Yeats. Also, perhaps, for having written the poem that inspired Debussy's ever-popular musical tour-de-force, "The Afternoon of a Faun."

In "Sea Breeze" Mallarmé writes:

La chair est triste, hélas! et j'ai lu tous les livres.
Fuir! là-bas fuir! Je sens que des oiseaux sont ivres
D'être parmi l'écume inconnue et les cieux!
Rien, ni les vieux jardins reflétés par les yeux
Ne retiendra ce cœur qui dans la mer se trempe.
O nuits! ni la clarté déserte de ma lampe
Sur le vide papier que la blancheur défend
Et ni la jeune femme allaitant son enfant.
Je partirai! Steamer balançant ta mâture,

Lève l'ancre pour une exotique nature!
Un ennui, désolé par les cruels espoirs,
Croit encore à l'adieu suprême des mouchoirs!
Et, peut-être, les mâts, invitant les orages
Sont-ils de ceux qu'un vent penche sur les naufrages
Perdus, sans mâts, sans mâts, ni fertiles îlots…
Mais, ô mon cœur, entends le chant des matelots!

I arbitrarily render it as:

Away from grieving bodies, well-thumbed books,
dour dungeons of disapproving looks,
gardens of jealous gods and jostling vendors,
forbidden fruits and serpents with agendas,
lactating wives, blank pages: Elope
from the relentless cruelty of hope,
growing shadows that end the day,
away! Between the spume and spray
inebriated birds dip and bob freely:
forget French, pick up Swahili.
True, for all their siren calls
sea breezes may play you false.
Ships wreck, isles sink, and sharks devour,
there may be no auspicious hour,
no second place, no honourable mention,
no blue lagoon, swooping birds, no redemption
from playing out existence's grim string —
but listen, listen to the sailors sing.

It cannot be called a translation, obviously, but it is a variation on Mallarmé's theme in English, which is how I submit it to the reader. By the way, *Mais, ô mon cœur, entends le chant des matelots!"* is good advice. Despite storms, shipwrecks, and other outrages of nature, the sailors sing. Sea shanties do not eliminate the vicissitudes of the voyage but they are, and therefore have, by definition, the last word.

Spitteler

THE SWISS POET CARL Spitteler (1845–1924) was much honoured
in his lifetime, but even being awarded the Nobel Prize for liter-
ature did little to spread his name and works beyond his own
period and culture. Today he is hardly a household name even
among German-speaking readers, despite his poetry, plays, and
journalism having been enthusiastically received by his contem-
poraries. His story illustrates that it is easier to be compared to
Homer and Milton — which Spitteler was, by serious scholars —
than to find an audience.

Spitteler was only sixteen when he first tried his hand at
writing for the stage. He was seventeen when he began dabbling
in poetry, eighteen when he approached the study of law, and
twenty when he switched to theology in Zurich. His early
teachers in Basel included Jacob Burckhardt — not a bad start
for a fifteen-year-old. It is hard to say, of course, if the teenager
learned much from the discoverer — some say, inventor — of
the Renaissance, though the classical theme of Spitteler's first
epic, *Prometheus und Epimetheus,* indicates a possible influence.

The poet worked for eight years as a tutor in Russia and Finland, as well as a teacher in an exclusive girl's school, before returning to Zurich and embarking on a career in journalism. He became an acquaintance and something of a protégé of the eminent Swiss writer Gottfried Keller — by then collecting rather than creating his distinguished oeuvre — and at the age of thirty-eight married one of his former students, Maria Op den Hoof. The next ten years were his most productive period.

Arguably, one person who did Spitteler no favour was his father-in-law who, upon dying in 1893, left the forty-eight-year-old poet-playwright-journalist financially independent. While one cannot say that Spitteler never did a lick of work again — he certainly produced several plays and volumes of poetry — the inheritance relieved him of the necessity to connect with an audience and/or posterity. Instead of popular success, he pursued a Ph.D. and the Nobel Prize, achieving the first in 1905 and the second in 1919. He merited the prize, at least more than some who received it both before and after him, but a politically sensitive Nobel-committee may also have given a candidate from neutral Switzerland an edge over a former belligerent. He died four years later, at the age of seventy-nine.

Spitteler is unabashedly high culture. As a poet-playwright, he is intelligent, visionary, sardonic, versatile, mythopoeic, and largely unread. "The Kindly Procurator" is my take on his theme.

THE KINDLY PROCURATOR

The Procurator was a kindly soul,
And more than kindly, he was practical,
Spreading the word through his vast estate,
Commanding all under his thrall:
"Men have value, like fine jars. Do not break them.
No whip, no chain, just question and explain.
Let captives choose their own work, and the gain
Will be mine. Don't cut against the grain.
A happy slave is a productive slave."

As new captives were led to his enclave
The Procurator questioned them himself
In tones benign, and dignified, and grave
Making sure none was being coerced,
Abused or injured in his pride,
Poorly husbanded, tossed aside.
"A boot-maker? You'll make me boots.
A shepherd? You'll tend my flocks.
Physician, cure my tenant's pox.
Seamstress, my tunic needs darning.
A stonemason? You'll carve my granite."

One was left. "And what about you?"
The slave raised his eyes until their glances met.
"I was the King." A moment's pause ensued.
Captives and overseers held their breath.
The Roman, with a man's fate in his hand,
And reversed fortune's haughty hate in view,
Sober but merciful, turned to his retinue
And said: "Put this one to death."

Karinthy

A CHILDHOOD FRIEND ONCE remarked that the superb clown of Hungarian literature did not come by his humour honestly. Born in 1887 of rather humdrum parents, no one would have foreseen that Frigyes (Frederick) Karinthy would die in 1938 as one of his country's most entertaining writers. His popularity persists to this day, but few people would describe him as a poet. The humorist in him overshadowed the considerable gift he had for other literary genres. If the man who dreamt that he was two cats that played with each other also wrote memorable poems and intriguing short stories, they went relatively unnoticed. The combined voices of Stephen Leacock, A. A. Milne, James Thurber, Mark Twain, Jerome K. Jerome, and P. G. Wodehouse spoke so loudly and eloquently in Karinthy that readers rarely noticed he had a voice resembling Alexander Pope's, Jonathan Swift's, and Robert Browning's as well.

In my version of "Magyar Jacobins, *1795*" the first four stanzas are a heavily condensed summary of Karinthy's long quasi-symphonic poem that describes the conspiracy and trial of the Abbot Martinovics. The last three stanzas are free translations of the final movement — "The Execution" — of Karinthy's actual poem. I modified slightly the spelling of Hungarian names for the benefit of English-speaking readers who want to read the poem for themselves as poems should be read: out loud. (Thus Martinovics becomes Martinovich, etc.)

THE MAGYAR JACOBINS, 1795

The winds of France blew and inspired,
the staid Magyar plains gaped, impressed.
Martinovich, abbot, conspired.
Martinovich, abbot, confessed:

"Judges, we were men of the cloth,
not of the sword, rebellious kind…
If, all the same, we hatched a plot
it was the wind to blame, the wind.

"The wind whispered for us to bring
— lawyers, clerics, men of the pen —
Vienna of demure Danube
freedom from Paris-by-the-Seine.

"Yes, I admit, we spoke, we wrote,
we translated La Marseillaise…
Now we implore the Emperor,
have mercy on us if you please."

Sigray was the first go.
Szolártsik stumbled as he climbed
the steps. Õz shoved the priest,
Szentmarjay fought, Hajnóczy cried.

Martinovich — old notes reveal —
was comatose, beyond alarm.
On the scaffold the axe-man tried
to hold him underneath the arm.

Hair disheveled, he meekly dropped
upon the executioner's chest
his old child's head, then snuggled up
to the block moist with clotting blood.

Ábrányi

EMIL ÁBRÁNYI COULD NOT make the leap between the nineteenth century in which he was born (1851) and the twentieth in which he died at the age of sixty-nine (1920). As a result, his name is barely known today in Hungary, the country where as a young man he was one of the most popular poets. In other countries he is not known at all. Ironically, the poet whose translations of Hugo, Byron, and especially Edmond Rostand are to this day the gold standard in Hungary (theatre-goers may not know Ábrányi's name, but they can think of Rostand's *Cyrano de Bergerac* only in his words) has himself never been translated into any foreign language as far as I know.

It has been suggested that it is difficult to translate poetry much above the translator's own class; a featherweight cannot tackle a heavyweight, and so on. I think this confuses poetry with pugilism. As a poet, Ábrányi was certainly not in Hugo's or Byron's league, though he was arguably in a league above Rostand's. (Another irony: Rostand may be two leagues south of Byron, but his *Cyrano* is still played all over the world, whereas *Manfred*, Byron's *magnum opus*, is rarely if ever revived even in Britain, let alone elsewhere.) Perhaps Ábrányi was handicapped in the posterity-game, not only by never making the transition from Goethesque *Sturm-und-Drang* romanticism to any branch of *fin de siècle* modernity — although there were many to choose from and Ábrányi knew them all — but also by not being aggressively ambitious. Having the funds and social standing to be above it all is not necessarily conducive to staying ahead in the competition for library space. As the scion of a prominent land-owning family — the Eördöghs of Szentgyörgyábrány; he called himself Ábrányi after the ancestral estate — and as an opposition member of parliament, the poet was aggressive only about his patriotism.

"Ribbons for a Flag" is a conversation inspired by Ábrányi's theme, as expressed in the first four lines. The next four lines are my variations.

RIBBONS FOR A FLAG

The patriot's ribbon:

Seeing my country bereft of freedom
is sheer torture, a curse.
But seeing freedom, bereft of my county
is infinitely worse.

The exile's ribbon:

Countries are nice. A dime a dozen.
It's freedom that isn't growing on trees.
Countries abound. Liberty doesn't.
Better to have no country, and be free.

Anonymous

THEY COME IN VARIOUS forms: poems and songs whose origins are lost in the mists of time, or lost just as surely in the mists of one's own mind. Some have been authored and abandoned by one person; some by many. Some of unclaimed authorship are virtually unknown; others are more popular than duly accredited poems. Some are on permanent exhibition; others live in the back alleys of the culture, like stray cats. We will look briefly at both kinds.

Certain folk ballads, like "Bullfrog" and "Old Judge," have found their way into the repertory of gypsy bands. These quasifolk tunes have tremendous popular appeal in East and Central Europe. They are offered incessantly, live and recorded, in concerts, in radio programs, and, most annoyingly, in restaurants. If their anonymous authors ever received royalties, they would be in the pink.

Far from being a devotee of the genre, once I quipped that communism was the minor reason for my fleeing Budapest in 1956; the major reason was gypsy music. Having said this, I must concede some folk ballads have a kind of hardboiled sentimentality that is difficult to resist. This bittersweet amalgam has made "Bullfrog" (or "goat-frog" as the warty old *rana catesbeiana* is called in Hungarian) a favorite encore piece in traditional nightspots, with "Never Stole a Thing …" ("*Nem loptam még életemben …*") not far behind. Gypsy musicians rarely sing; the lead violinist, called *primás,* coaxes the lyrics from the throats of patrons, mostly middle-aged men, in various stages of inebriation. These brave vocalists are deep not only into their cups but in the throes of exquisite male self-pity. Still, such sing-along performances (usually off-key) are not the less heartfelt for being ridiculous.

My versions render the first stanzas of the ballads faithfully into English, followed by variations on their respective themes. The second and third stanzas of "Bullfrog" as well as "Old Judge" are flights of fancy, albeit composed in the manner of the original text — in short, they are literary caricatures.

BULLFROG

Well, the bullfrog clambered up the
willow tree.
To the very highest branches
climbed up he.
It wouldn't add up this way, that way,
no way would it add up twice.
Not unless it was somebody
else's wife.

Every time I happen to have
had a drop,
I take a deep breath till the good air
puffs me up.
In the arbour by the harbour
hop by hop
I climb a fancy weeping willow
to the top.

Bullfrogs have no fear that they might
burn in hell.
Nor have I, as far as passers-
by can tell.
Sit in my tree croaking smugly
come what may,
till a passing heron gulps me
down one day.

OLD JUDGE

"Never stole a thing, your Honour,
only a mare from the manor."
Old judge had me clapped in iron,
my sweetheart, she is still crying.
      Damn the law!

"Robbed no person, God's my witness,
only a drunk, outside Deak's Nest."
Old judge sent me up the river.
Gentle Jesus, please deliver.
      Damn the law!

Never took a life, I swear it.
Save old judge's — he could spare it.
Paid a lawyer to defend me,
at sundown they will still hang me.
      Damn the law!

The folk song "Spring Breezes" *("Tavaszi szél …")* is simply a translation from the Hungarian.

SPRING BREEZES

Spring breezes blow, streams are cresting,
my flower, my flower.
Birds are choosing mates for nesting,
my flower, my flower.

Who will be the mate to fit you,
my flower, my flower?
You nest with me, I'll nest with you,
my flower, my flower …

Forgotten

A LINE I READ somewhere has lingered in my mind, marking the grave of a fallen poem. Like the tomb of the Unknown Soldier, "the black train black goes black black shuffling through" is a humble monument to what used to be my memory.

The line came at the end of a poem, but I cannot recall any of the lines that preceded it. I do not know what they were about, who wrote them, or where they appeared. My search through anthologies, periodicals, and the Internet yielded no clue. The source of "the black train black goes black black shuffling through" was lost to me, but the words kept echoing in my ears. In the end, not being able to get rid of the line, I composed a short poem to go with it, which I offer here in homage to the Unknown Poet.

THE BLACK TRAIN

Like sparks along the railroad, flies the time.
Somebody wrote this line; I don't know who.
Is it poison? Anemic anodyne?
"The black train black goes black black shuffling through."

Somebody wrote this line; I don't know why
it stays with me, still fizzling like a stein
of bitter brew. In the mind's serpentine
the black train black goes black black shuffling by.

Old footage in a can marked monochrome.
It's too fragile to watch. I don't know how
we missed each other. Waited for you. Now,
the black train black goes black black shuffling home.

POETS, ALPHABETICALLY

~~

POETS, BY LANGUAGE

TO HEAR A SAMPLE from *The Jonas Variations* read aloud, scan this QR code:

Or visit www.cormorantbooks.com/thejonasvariations

ACKNOWLEDGEMENTS

POETRY COLLECTIONS OFTEN LIST work previously published in magazines and such. My list will be short, for most poems in this book appear in print for the first time. The exceptions are in my 1993 collection, *The East Wind Blows West*, published by Ronsdale Press, which did include earlier versions of some variations on George Faludy's themes. A draft of the Faludy-Villon ballad "Danse Macabre" appeared in John Robert Colombo's 2006 anthology, *Two For Faludy*. Eventually, in 2009, Boris Castel printed my imitations or adaptations of Apollinaire, Heredia, Verlaine, Goethe, and Labé poems in his handsome summer issue of *The Queen's Quartely* as excerpts from what was then a work-in-progress.

The Jonas Variations is not only the Jonas variations. Books are collaborative efforts, and this one owes its existence to the advice and labour of many friends. My thanks go to the late George Faludy first, who introduced me to the genre and gave me the benefit of his comments on several poems in this book. I am grateful to other friends who did likewise: the novelist and essayist Stephen Vizinczey and his wife, Gloria; the columnist David Warren; my former wife (and editor) Barbara Amiel; and especially the novelist and poet Guy Gavriel Kay, my writing partner during our broadcasting years, who gave generous blocks of his time and attention to earlier drafts of this manuscript.

Foreign languages are tricky. Generous friends helped by casting a cold eye on some texts, or arranged for me to rely on the kindness of strangers. I am very grateful for this and other assistance to Pierre Lemieux, Patrick Luciani, Claudia Zuccato, Professor John MacCormack and the Master of Massey College, John Fraser.

The book took a long time to find a home. Along with my agents at Westwood Creative Artists, Linda McKnight, and the indefatigable Chris Casuccio, it was my former publisher and editor, Anna Porter, who became a combination of marriage broker and midwife to the project. Another friend, the copyright lawyer Grace Westcott, did her invaluable share of facilitation as well.

Poetry, among other things, means digging for *le mot juste*. At Cormorant Books my editor, Robyn Sarah, handed me two perfect words on a platter. Had she done nothing else — and she did plenty — she would have earned my gratitude. So would Marc Côté, a publisher who understands that books do not have to be down market to be user-friendly.

For the cover design and photography my thanks go to Angel Guerra, and for interior design my thanks to Tannice Goddard.

My principal collaborators have been the poets whose spirit I have tried to conjure up in a literary séance. Thanking them would be presumptuous because they did not write their poems for my purposes, but to the extent that I succeeded, the credit belongs to them. To the extent that I failed, I owe them my profound apologies, and pray that they are forgiving souls.